Newbie Friendly

List Building Secrets

12 Free & Dirt Cheap (but Proven Effective) Ways to Quickly Build a Responsive Email List

(They'll be people who look forward to buying from you ... even if you're just starting out online!)

ISBN: 9781549563720
© 2017 Ben Settle
Published by MakeRight Publishing, Inc.

WAIT!

Before reading, please take a second and go to:

www.BenSettle.com

... to access the hundreds of FREE tips and hours of audio content waiting there for you. Plus, if you join the mailing list you will also get a free (digital pdf) issue of the prestigious ($97/month) "Email Players" newsletter.

Disclaimers
Please Read Carefully

ONE FINAL THING: The URL's in this book are subject to change and may not work at any given time, depending on the website.

Table of Contents

Chapter 1
How the "Most Connected" Man Online Builds His List with Email, YouTube, and the Gift of Gab

BEN SETTLE: Hello everybody this is Ben Settle of BenSettle.com. And today I'm talking to a friend of mine David Dutton who's been called the most connected man on the Internet. He's had a lot success setting up joint ventures and business deals with people of power and influence. He's done deals with the legendary Jim Straw, Willie Crawford, Joe Vitale, David Frey, and Michael Senoff, even Jessie Conners, star of the Donald Trump's, *The Apprentice*. These are people most of us only read about in many cases, but David has been able to sort of move his way into their lives and strike up profitable deals using some really simple techniques we're going to talk about today. David are you there?

DAVID DUTTON: I am.

BEN SETTLE: I want to start this off with sort of challenging you on something. Okay, what makes you the most connected man on the Internet, and how did you develop this skill?

DAVID DUTTON: Let me just tell your listeners the fact that after this phone call you'll be able to do this, okay. Now, you may have to listen to it over and over again just to get the confidence if you're not that self-confident, but you will be able to do this. I'm going to share with you what I do and how I do it. I'm from Tennessee. I'm a Southern boy, you probably can tell with the Southern accent and everything. Well, I'm 29, but at 16-years old I always knew I was an entrepreneur. I just knew I wasn't going to work for anybody. But I was wrestling with what I was going to do after high school. I just wasn't sure, I didn't like school that much, because I just wanted to go out and make money even at that age. I was working for Garden Plaza Hotel which is in Murphysboro, Tennessee. It's now Double Tree Hotel. As a clerk, I was making $6 - $7 an hour, I believe. I was wrestling with my life, had a lot of personal things going on. One of the guests in there, as I'm just kind of day dreaming which I do a lot, I saw one of our guests walk by, a doctor, and it hit me. I was like, "Wait a minute. I don't have to go to Law School or Med School. All I have to do is know one. And if I just hang out with them I can pick up the phone and they'll help me out if I give value to their life." You just can't call a buddy and ask favors all the time if you're not giving him returns, giving value into your buddy's life. So that changed my life, but I didn't get use that, Ben, until like years later, but that still to this day, even at 29 years old, was an "ah-ha" moment. That changed my life, because it changed my thinking. I went to a little small Bible college in Chattanooga, Tennessee. And when I was home for break at 21-years old I was trying to get a sales job. I was very hungry, I had read a book called, *How to Master the Art of Selling,* by Tom Hopkins, changed my life. I knew I wanted a straight commission job. This was '97, '98, '99 around there, when cell phones were so huge as far as you could make a lot of money in it. So people had them, but there was still a lot of money to be had selling them.

I walked into Absolute Wireless in Murphysboro, Tennessee, I said, "Hey, can I get a straight commission job, do you all have those?" They hired me on the spot. I learned how to sell Nextel and all this. I drove what I call a 1986 "ghetto-fabulous" Honda Accord. And I didn't have any money if it broke down, so I didn't want it to break down. So I didn't want to cold call. I didn't want to go driving and parking and trying to stop with these businesses and try to sell them cell phones, so I said, "Okay, wait a minute. I got a directory." Some type of Chamber of Commerce newspaper. It even had Nashville businesses as well. I started calling, I was making like a 100 calls a day. And I would do 90 percent of my selling right over the phone. By the time I got to them I was showing them the phone, and they were signing the contract, and I was done. And I made $100, $200, $300, $400. I was making about $3,000 working about 20 hours a week. Doing that changed my life. That's when I started getting good on the phone and started networking a little bit. A buddy of mine approached me about doing a barter business. Well he's a little technical geek type guy and very intelligent, but he's not a networker or anything. He had a Chinese connection that we could get connections in China. And what we were going to do was approach American drug companies that just got drugs and devices approved by the FDA that wanted to sell their stuff in China.

We would approach them; we would call them up and say, "Hey, do you want to sell it? You give us a percentage of the deal and we'll broker the deal for you." So anyway, my buddies weren't going to call anybody, so I was like, "Okay, give me a piece of the action I'll call." So, I was 24-years old calling Fortune 100 CEOs, CFOs, COOs out of my dorm room, from a cell phone number, no website, no one to hand your number, nothing. Just calling them like I owned it. I just happened to have a surplus of confidence. I knew that they were going to do business with me. Did they all do business with me? No, actually none of them did except for one. Now, to sell your drugs in China I found out, I didn't know about this, but it takes about $8 million to get drugs through the Chinese government. My cut was going to be like $80,000 out of $8 million. This was good at 24. I'm like, "Okay, that's cool. You know, that could start my real estate business and that type of thing, so I'm all right with that." So that's why I was doing it. Well, I call this one company and I'll never forget it Biosensors out of California. I'm on the phone I say, "Hey, are you interested?" They're like, "Yeah, I think we are." It was a good call, but no deal or anything, especially not on the first phone call, because you got to build a trust. Well, I'm driving on I-75 in Chattanooga, Tennessee; I can still see exactly where I was, when I was riding in the passenger seat with my buddy in his Volkswagen Golf. And I get a call about 8:30 on my cell phone said, "Hi, this is Chuck Wong from Biosensors." It was like an Asian guy. And I was like, "Yes, what can I do for you?" He said, "I heard you talked to Bob earlier and we're very interested in your proposal. We wanted to see if we could fly you down to California next week." I didn't say this, but I was just like, "Oh my God. Are you serious?" So I said, "I don't have my planner with me. I'm not sure I'm out of the office. Can I call you back?" He said, "Yes, please call me back." So I just got my buddy to contact our Asian guy and they started networking, because I don't fly. That's kind of my trademark at mostconnectedmarketer.com is how I do all these deals from Murphysboro, Tennessee without getting on an airplane. I don't meet anybody at seminars, because most of them are across the country, and I have a flying phobia. So I'm not going to California, that's crazy.

So anyway, the deal started rolling and everything. Long story short, I learned a very valuable lesson with contracts and lawyers. You need them, you need both. So I got squeezed out of the deal. Some people are like, "Okay, so you didn't put an $8 million deal together." Well actually I did put the $8 million deal together; I just didn't get any money out of it. But that was such a confidence booster I could do anything. At 22 I found people were making money on the Internet. So I translated that into making money, like I was terrified to build a website, because I'm not a technical guy, so I'd use those same networking skills I learned at the cell phone job, the import/export business that we created. I took those skills and I applied it to Internet marketing and started trying to broker deals for big dogs. I like to share that whole story so people understand my mindset and where I came from, so they can do the same thing.

BEN SETTLE: There was no previous connection here; I mean you just started from scratch. Just a regular guy started from scratch and now you're doing business with all these other people and you didn't have any help getting it, and you just kind of used some street smarts.

DAVID DUTTON: I didn't have anything. I was broke as a joke at the time, but I had ambition, and

I knew the alternative was to get a job and I didn't want to do that stuff. I mean, I had good part-time jobs at times, but I knew there was something more like Michael Dell did it out of is dorm room. Bill Gates quit. If they do it why can't I? You just have to have confidence, and I expect them to do business with me. Like that's another thing, like when I talk about mindset that it is just rah-rah, no. Like I expect people to talk to me, now some people are like, "Hey, man that's like pretty cocky." You have to believe that. If you don't believe that you have value that you can bring, if I'm trying to do a deal with Ben Settle and I don't feel like I can bring value into Ben's life, you're not going to network with David Dutton. So that's how I feel. And I expect them to view me on their level. Even though I was 24-years old and I was talking to that 40, 50-year old guy that were probably making half a million a year with stock options. Give me time and I'm going to be there. It's just not an option it's just time, I'm just young.

BEN SETTLE: So one of your ways of doing this is you don't even bother unless you're going to bring something valuable to the table. That's kind of like you're in with these guys.

DAVID DUTTON: Yeah, now I try now to only contact people that I'm fans of. It works, I'm getting an endorsement in a major newsletter next week, and I'm going to show you how I did it. I'm a fan of a guy named Dr. Andy Williams. I heard about him about a year or two ago. He has a software called Keyword Results Analyzer. I do keyword research for people to help them get rankings really high in Google, and Yahoo, and all that. I used his software to filter keywords. Basically, I'm just a big fan of it. I wanted an endorsement in his newsletter, so you know what I did? I opened up Camtasia which is a screen capture software where it captures my computer screen, and I filmed and I put an audio to the video. Basically, I opened up the software, show people how I use it, and show them the results of a travel site I own, and just how I'm such a fan of Dr. Andy Williams. I put it on YouTube, which is free. I went to his support desk I filled out a support desk with the subject line, "KRA success story." I just said, "Hey, Andy I just want to let you know I did a case study about my success with your software and its right here on YouTube so everybody can see it. And it gets ranked in Google, blah, blah, the whole nine yards." Well, what did I do? Did I try to pitch him anything? No. Did I try to sell him anything? No, I didn't do anything, but give value. He said, "Hey, great idea, love the video. I'm going to mention you in my newsletter next week." Now, here's the cool thing. On that video, I have mentioned my links to my other websites, keywordresearchnerd.com, and mostconnectedmarketer.com. I had those all throughout the entire video.

BEN SETTLE: Is that kind of how you ended up doing deals with, for example, a guy like David Frey who, again, I'm sure he's not the most accessible guy in the world.

DAVID DUTTON: David Frey was one of the hardest people to contact. People asked me who's hard? Jesse Conners from The Apprentice was easier than David Frey. It took me like three years more with David Frey, but I'm the only person that's gotten four endorsements to his list of over 52,000 people and I didn't even ask for it. I didn't even know the times he was going to do it. He did it about three weeks ago, and I didn't even know about it. But I've done stuff to catch his attention. If you type in David Dutton in Google, type in David Dutton magic ball video, I'll pull up. He did a video about a ball I sent in the mail. So yeah, basically I just try to give value to these people. He can use that video in his marketing on his sales later.

BEN SETTLE: I think that's a good point. This is something that I know anyone, I mean, this has happened to me on a smaller scale, but I know it happens though to people who have much bigger influence than me. And I know they get annoyed by it. People will just email them or they'll call them and just say, "Hey, want to joint venture?" Or, "Hey, I got this new product and man, I think you should just send it out to your list." If you give value first and you strike up a relationship like you're talking about it's a lot better.

DAVID DUTTON: Oh, exactly. Now Andy already knew who I was, because I've talked to him before, but I can promise you he definitely knows who David Dutton is now. And do I approach him later on? Which I may or may not, I don't have an ulterior motive. I just wanted to do it, because I'm a fan.

BEN SETTLE: No ulterior motives you just try to give him some value, and say hi, and that's it. And there's no "I want to get something from you." There's just "I want to help you." And I guess the feeling is, "Hey, maybe someday we'll do some business and maybe we won't, but I just want to let you know I'm a fan and if you ever need any help..." Is that kind of what you're talking about here?

DAVID DUTTON: That is it. Whoever's listening to this rewind that and listen to it over again, because that's what I do. I might not benefit now, but six months down the road I may or I can go and ask a favor, because they remember me from six months ago. And I hook people up. I invite people to call me; I give my private cell phone number which nobody does. Mine's posted all over the Internet, but no one does. When people get Most Connected Marketer (www.mostconnectedmarketer.com), I invite people to call me. I don't even pitch them like I should. You would think I'm a nonprofit organization, because I don't even pitch people hardly. I build a relationship with them; sometimes we do a deal, sometimes we don't. But then like now, next time I send emails they listen to them more, because I actually answer my phone.

BEN SETTLE: The fact that you're even accessible by phone, that kind of makes you stick out. I mean, just having the option to call you makes you stick out.

DAVID DUTTON: Oh, yeah that's funny you say that, because most people don't even call me. But I guarantee in their mind, exactly what you're talking about, I guarantee that 10-foot wall that might be standing in between us is like two feet tall now.

BEN SETTLE: You and I have talked about that before, the 10 foot wall mind set. Can you explain that a little bit?

DAVID DUTTON: Okay. If I want to sell something to Ben Settle, whatever it is, I visualize there is a 10-foot brick wall right between us. And for Ben to hand me his Visa, and that's what I want at the end of the day, because that's what puts food on my table, makes my car payments, and pays off my student loan debt, and all that stuff. I have to make sure that wall is like two feet tall, so you can step over it and come to my side, and actually hand me his Visa. Now, how do I do that? Well, I do that by playing good offense and defense. I have a little strategy I teach my clients to play good defense. I get testimonials, case studies, the colors of your website, the way your brochure or the way you present yourself, the whole nine yards. If you got good testimonials they might drop three feet down, so the walls only seven feet down. Oh, okay, you have a really killer guarantee where people can't lose if they hire you. Okay, that might drop it down another four feet, so now it's only like two feet tall and Ben can step over and hand me his Visa.

BEN SETTLE: Now, do you apply that same concept, for example, when you do business with Jessie Conners of the Apprentice and maybe some others. Is that sort of the same concept? Even if you're not necessarily selling...?

DAVID DUTTON: I am selling. I'm selling David Dutton every phone call. Every relationship is David Dutton. Okay, so I'm selling something, whether it's the concept of David Dutton or a broker product, or service, or whatever if I'm talking to an actual prospect that's going to buy something from me. If I'm approaching Jessie Conners, or David Frey, or Willie Crawford, or Joe Vitale, or anybody, or any of those guys, Bob Burg of Endless Referrals, all those guys. So I'm contacting them, there's a 10 foot wall in between us, and then for me to break it down. Well, first of all I've broke down the wall a little bit by an email I came out with by accident. I started crafting a certain email. I have an email with a certain subject line and a certain way I write emails. I pretty much talk to whoever I want to. I mean, it's not 100 percent, because life's not 100 percent, but it works enough to where I meet a lot of people. And so I use email to break down that 10 foot wall before they even talk to me on the phone.

BEN SETTLE: You don't just contact people out of the blue on the phone. If they don't email you back or call you, you just don't even deal with them.

DAVID DUTTON: No, I'm done. I got other things to do.

BEN SETTLE: So you're only dealing with people who are already interested in you, or anything about you, or whatever it is that you want to talk about?

DAVID DUTTON: Yeah. You got it. I have an email, every now and then, it's like one percent of my time I've ever just picked up the phone and contacted somebody. Even if I could've, even if I had Kwame Jackson from The Apprentice's cell phone number. Or David Frey's private cell phone number. I just didn't do it. I just don't, because it's weird. It's like you're overstepping that social norm as they call it in Psychology. The social norm, the weirdness factor goes up. I use email to contact them first. And I structure my email with certain psychological, I guess, triggers. There's a great book on influence, *The Psychology of Persuasion.* It has the six basic core factors that motivate anybody on this planet, and I used it in email first. The favorite one that I have stressed to everybody is social proof. Social proof is basically another terminology; a slang terminology is the bandwagon effect. And basically, you'll follow a herd, you'll follow a group. One example is if you're coming off an airline, I love this Jeff Walker gave this analogy one time on a social proof first call. He said, "You're coming off an airplane and you don't know where to go get your luggage, because you've never been to that airport before. But all of a sudden out of the 30 group of strangers that just got off the airplane with you, you see like 25 of them or like 23 of them start going off to the left. And what are you going to do? You're probably going to follow the 23 people, because they're probably going to get the same thing that you're looking for, their luggage." And another terminology is called drinking the kool-aid. And that became famous with the Jim Jones cult. He got like 200 some people to commit a mass suicide, because they started watching other people in this group do something, and then everybody finally just did it. And they committed suicide. And you think, "Well, that can't happen." Well, yes it can actually. You can impact the way people think. I use social proof. Actually, the email that I send out, the second paragraph, I use social proof in it. And I want people to know that I hang out with other big shots that they know. So that's kind of like a social proof. Another one's scarcity, you want to limit yourself. I don't buy that as far as phone. I tend to go the other way as far as my networking. I'm very available, but you want to limit the quantity of a product, limit maybe access to you, different things like that. Make it scarce, because your value goes up. There are a lot of different factors, but social proof is probably my favorite.

BEN SETTLE: Let's say you were just starting out and you didn't know anyone. How would you use social proof? I mean, you just wait until you've gotten the first connection with someone before you use it or...?

DAVID DUTTON: I don't think I could use social proof right off the top of my head, I don't think I could use it yet. I would go a different route. What I would do, I would learn to give something in that email. If I was starting out with zero connections I would try to like, if I had bought your product or something, I would try to give you a case study of how I used it and how it changed my life or something.

BEN SETTLE: Which everybody appreciates that has a product. I mean, how can you ignore someone who does that.

DAVID DUTTON: Exactly. That's killer, because guess what? Everybody has an ego. You know what? I didn't even think about that. That's one of my big strategies. Most people have an ego, that's another reason why I like to stroke it. So I stroke their ego, and I'm sincere too. Keep in mind, I'll only contact people that I actually like. I do research on people before I contact them.

BEN SETTLE: You're not advocating, "Look, just find out a few things about them, maybe buy their product and then."

DAVID DUTTON: No, you can't. It doesn't work that way. Its interest, I feel like I have sales ability, and you don't have to. Don't think anyone listening to this, "Okay, no wonder you do, because you have sales ability." No, you can do this in your local town or International like I do either one. But you can use it locally as well, but you do not have to be a salesman. But God gifted me with, I guess, a gift of gab. But what's interesting is it's almost a blessing and curse, because if I don't believe in something you would think I was like the most introverted person in the entire planet, because I can't fake it. And I'm not a new age guy at all, but I can feel it if I'm in person, and I actually can feel it kind of over the phone, but it's really good in person. But I can feel what another person's feeling like. Not to be weird or anything, I'm not a new age guy or anything. There's energy around us that I can't explain it, maybe people more educated than I am can, but I can tell you it's there, because I can feel it when I'm selling or even when I'm on the phone with someone I can build rapport with people. And they can feel, even possibly in an email too, they can get that feeling. I can tell when people try to contact me, and I try to get a lot of people to contact me, because that's how I became the most connected man on the Internet. But sometimes you can smell like, "Hey, this guy's like a loser." This guy's trying to pitch me on whatever it is he's pitching, and he shouldn't be. He should be giving me something. Don't waste somebody's time whether it's the Mayor in small town, USA or it's Joe Vitale, or whoever.

BEN SETTLE: When you made the deal with Jessie Conners from The Apprentice. How did that work? Did you send the email? Did you do exactly what you're saying here, you sent the email, you used your technique, and you were a fan, and all that? Is that exactly how you did that?

DAVID DUTTON: Yeah, actually just about almost word for word. When I launched my first book which is called, *David Dutton's Internet Empires, How Average People Are Making Money Online.* I ended up getting lazy with it. I wanted it to hit the Best Seller List. Well, I wanted to get a celebrity to help endorse my book, because that ups my value if I can get a celebrity to endorse my book.

BEN SETTLE: It's the social proof and all that.

DAVID DUTTON: Yeah, social proof absolutely. Because David Dutton's hanging out with a celebrity. Basically, I was looking for a celebrity, that their 15 minutes was up, wanted to start it over again and they were going to be cheap, because I didn't want to pay any money or very little money. So, I was like, "Who do I contact?" And I was like, "Wait a minute, Apprentice, okay their reality TV shows up. They're on like season three now." I mean I was like, "Jessie Conners." She is so sincere. She is very nice. She is very strong, like independent as far as like a good business person and everything. Don't let her fool you or whatever. But she got on there at 22-years old, but I just like her from the show.

BEN SETTLE: So you were a fan?

DAVID DUTTON: Yeah, I really was, I was a fan. I was like, "Wow, she was a cool girl."

BEN SETTLE: You were rooting for her to actually get it, probably.

DAVID DUTTON: Yeah, totally. I felt like I was like her. That's another thing. I felt like I have a commonality with that person. She was just like a regular person like in Minnesota doing well in real estate, which that was her thing. And here I am building my Internet marketing thing and stuff, and that's my passion. So, I'm like, you know me I have like a commonality. So, I used my email, I found one of her websites; I had to do research and found out what she was doing and contacted her. And then we exchanged emails, and it took a couple of weeks. She travels a lot doing seminars. Then we talked on the phone. And by that time, I've done this so many times, but I'm still shocked. I'm like, "It's really cool, I connected somebody that hung out with Donald Trump several times." I have a picture on my computer with her and Donald Trump, so that's pretty cool. One phone call away you're one person away from Donald Trump now, just from one person. Now, will I ever talk to Donald Trump? Who knows, I haven't tried contacting him, because I don't have anything I could bring value to Donald Trump's life right now. My goal is to get on the Donny Deutsch show. He's another guy I like. He's for the boot strap Entrepreneur, so that's why I want to be on his show one day. But I'll contact him, I have a strategy already in my mind I'm just not there yet to where I can bring the value to his show.

BEN SETTLE: There's this marketer Ken McCarthy do you know who he is?

DAVID DUTTON: Oh, yeah.

BEN SETTLE: He did this copywriting seminar a few years ago. It was a really good seminar and everything. His cousin did business with the Queen of England sort of on accident using almost your exact system.

DAVID DUTTON: Oh my God.

BEN SETTLE: She was just a regular person, just a regular ordinary person like the rest of us. His cousin, I guess, is a doctor or something, but basically lives in New Jersey, doesn't know anyone special or anything. But she apparently is into horses, and I think it was Halflinger horses or something. She was so into it that she kind of made her own calendar; just like someone would if they were into dogs they might make their own dog calendar or something. And she found out that the Queen of England was into the same kind of horses, so just for the fun of it she sent her one of the calendars. And low and behold one day the Queen of England called her up personally and just said, "I just loved your calendar. Come out and hang out with me at the Palace." And there she was, she actually went out there and hung out with the Queen of England. I don't know if they did business or not, but it so illustrates exactly what you've been saying here.

DAVID DUTTON: Oh, that's huge, yes.

BEN SETTLE: Let's kind of shift over to something else here, like the next step of the process. Okay, you sent the email out and let's say David Frey called you back. He's going to call you back and you know when he's going to call you back. What do you do to kind of prepare for your first time? I mean, you're used to it now, so it's probably not a big deal, but to someone who's never done this before what do you tell them?

DAVID DUTTON: First of all you're going to be nervous. You're flat out going to be nervous. And you're always going to get a little bit of jitters and stuff, but you're going to get a lot your first one or two, whether it's the Mayor of your town or David Frey, or anybody, Donald Trump, or whatever. Realize that they're just a person. God gave them the same organs that you have. They have the same 24 hours a day. They're just regular people, and they happen to be doing a certain thing in a certain industry, and they happen to be successful. Other than that, they're just like you. Number two; expect that they should be talking to you. If you're pitching something I would be very scared. I'd be terrified if they're calling me. Because you're about to be screwed, you're about to waste their time, and you're never going to have that relationship ever again, because you're branded like that now. Think about that you're on their level, and that you expect them to talk to you, because you have value. You're about to bring value that's about to rock their fricken world. You sparked their interest by using the email. And I use email to get them onto the phone, because my phone's my secret weapon, because I can bond with people very quickly.

BEN SETTLE: Have you ever tried besides email maybe sending a Federal Express letter or something? Would that work too?

DAVID DUTTON: If I really want to do business with Ben Settle and you're not reading your email, and I really, really am persistent and I want to do business with you I will get creative. Let me give you an example, I wish I could take credit for this, but Leo Quinn of leoquinn.com is a buddy of mine out of New York. He's a very good networker. He actually will send somebody a cell phone with prepaid minutes on it, like 20 minutes for $12. You can go to trackphone.com and do that. So if you're not answering me then I might send you a cell phone and tell you to call me. And that's like ridiculous. I haven't had to do that, because I'm fine with the results I get when I want to talk to people. And it gets easier, because another thing is, let's just say that I try to contact John Doe. And I just happen to realize that Ben Settle is friends with John Doe. Well, now it just got so much easier, because I'm going in the back door.

I'm sitting out on the porch drinking tea with them now, because Ben's been sitting there calling John Doe for me, "Hey listen you need to talk to this guy David Dutton."

BEN SETTLE: It's almost like the more you do this it's just like interest compounding on itself. It just gets easier and easier, and easier, because you know more and more people, and you have more of that social proof, and more of that endorsement. You have their friends and their network, and now you are just kind of getting into their inner circle one contact at a time.

DAVID DUTTON: Exactly. People buy from people they know, like, and trust. All you have to do is get people to know, like, and trust you. And if you give value then when you pick up the phone and call them for a favor, boom, done. It will happen, because you give, give, give, and stuff and word gets out.

BEN SETTLE: You mentioned you've written two books now. One of them I remember you said you've got with a bunch of millionaires and they actually wrote it for you. Well, how did that work?

DAVID DUTTON: Okay, here I am maybe 27-years old was sitting around. I had a nice time in Bible College even though it was Bible College I had a really good time. I spent a lot of money, so I ran up a lot of student loan debt. Well I didn't want to be 60-years old paying off student loan debt, so I said, "How can I make money?" So I said, "I'll just write a book, and I'll just make a lot of money selling the book, and then getting jobs off of the book for consulting and different things like that." I already had all these connections, so I said, "I'll tell you what, I'll just interview all these people." And I created a book called, *Internet Empires.* All I did was interview these people using my system in the Get Connected report (www.mostconnectedmarketer.com), literally word for word and the email and everything, and did interviews. I would take the interviews, I put famous people in there like Joe Vitale, who's been on Oprah, who's like a four-time Best Selling Author. He's been on Donnie Deutsch. He's been on Larry King. I put Willie Crawford in there who's a millionaire. I put Jeff Walker who has very few interviews on the entire Internet. I had him in my product. I put people like prominent in my niche. But I also, my passion, my true passion is teaching people how to make money on the Internet that are just average people that have two kids, a wife, and a mortgage, or even a second mortgage and they want to start an Internet business.

So, I put those people in there that are making money online as well. I would interview people, remember I don't fly I have a phobia, so I would interview people all across the world including. Iceland, Texas, all these people I've never seen before and probably never will. Don Peters who sold a missile silo on eBay, all those guys I emailed and interviewed them. As soon as I interviewed them I would send it over to these high school students. One of them is in Canada and one of them, I think, was in Romania. They would transcribe my interviews for me. I took the transcriptions and I paid people to edit my book for me. And then my publisher actually edited it and put the graphics on there. And, *David Dutton's Internet Empires, What These Nine People Can Teach You About Making Money Online. And there's my book.* I've gotten like over 20 something more interviews of people that I could literally do a book. I was actually going to do a five-book series, but it gets better, because the book sells for $16.95. You can't make a living unless you sell thousands and thousands of books every month if you're making $10 - $12 profit. But, let me tell you something, David Frey endorsed my book. That was my first endorsement. I made about $500 off of that deal in a day. I made I think $1,400 or $1,700 that day David Frey endorsed my book. Well, Ryan Lee, the famous ryanlee.com was a big-time marketer millionaire at age 34, personaltraineryou.com, yeah, all those guys, big guys, been on the Millionaire Blueprints Magazine. He calls me out of the blue and he says, "Hey, man this is Ryan Lee." I was like, "Hey." Is this the Ryan Lee? I was thinking this I didn't say that. I was like, "Oh, hey what's going on buddy?" And so we're talking and he says, "Man you got endorsed by David Frey and you write copy." And I'm like, "Yeah, I write copy." He said, "I probably have some projects for you pretty soon. You've got to be a good guy if David Frey endorses you." Did you see how that just happened?

BEN SETTLE: Right, it just had social proof again, and it came to you.

DAVID DUTTON: Exactly. Okay, now watch this. Watch what happens. Two days later I get an email from a Nick Osbourne. It says, "Hey listen, Ryan Lee referred me. I need some copy done." I said, "Okay." It turns out Nick Osbourne is like a big, big personal trainer in the strong man competition, like the World's Strongest Man Competition. He's in Ohio; he has a very successful weight training business. So he said he's training Phil Pfister, the World's Strongest Man. Anybody listening, next time you watch ESPN2 when they're throwing those cars around, those barrels, and carrying the cars, and all that stuff. There's a big blonde headed guy name Phil Pfister. He is the World's Strongest Man; he's the first American to win in 25 years. Him and Nick Osbourne train together and they filmed their workouts for 12 weeks and they want to put it on DVD's, so they did that. And they needed somebody to write copy. Well that was like a $400 copy job, but now look at my credibility. I have a client that is the World's Strongest Man and he's on ESPN2.

BEN SETTLE: Right. I mean, it just amazes me how that just multiplies on itself one at a time, and it just explodes and expands. Before you know it now you're a celebrity within some of these niches all because you were just doing these little things you've been talking about.

DAVID DUTTON: Yeah, that's it. There's no other secret, Ben, there's nothing. I literally in my book I write it like a journal entry and I supply what I'm telling you right now. I mean, this is basically it.

BEN SETTLE: Well, you know what's really interesting about this. You talked about how you interviewed them and then they basically wrote your book for you. Let's take this down to someone else's level. Maybe they're not in the making money business. Maybe they're just selling let's say a vitamin supplement or something. They could easily take that idea, interview a bunch of doctors and maybe even some celebrity nutritionists and do the exact same thing, with anything they're selling.

DAVID DUTTON: Oh totally. You could just go to town. I'm about to come out with a $7 product on how my uncle, my own uncle, made $18,000 on his first real estate deal. He lives in Portland, Tennessee, he's a former cop. He doesn't know anything about this stuff, and I'm going to interview him. Well, he's an expert, because he just made $18,000. He used to interview a doctor and deal with them. They don't know about marketing, you can create a product out of that stuff. I'm telling you, you need to become an author. That changed my life. An author of a CD, or a book, or whatever, and I don't even care if you actually sell one book. I can see it. I can feel it the way people talk to me, and I can see it in their eyes when they talk to me in person.

BEN SETTLE: And the amazing thing is you didn't even write the book.

DAVID DUTTON: I didn't write the book, no. The cover looks ridiculous, it's awesome. I've got some big shots in there. You better believe I dropped Joe Vitale's name. You better believe I tell people that he was on Larry King and Oprah, The World's Strongest Man guy, all these different things. I do that for credibility. That 10 foot wall just got to be one foot just because I, I call it dropping the hammer on people. You can drop the hammer. You make it so ridiculous that they can't say no. You just drop the hammer on him.

BEN SETTLE: Tell us about the magic ball. That was an incredible story.

DAVID DUTTON: It was pretty cool. I love it. In fact, I'm probably going to send out some this week, because I got some people I want to network with. But like a couple months ago seven o'clock in the morning I'm just like waking up, getting ready, eating a bowl of cereal, I see Good Morning America on. And they have an extra on there talking about, it was so crazy, the topic was how to increase employee retention or make employees feel better at work and stuff. And they had all these different things that you could do, had this expert on there. The very first item that they showed was this little rubber ball. When I say little, it's about as big as somebody's head. So, it's not necessarily little, but it's not huge. It's not as big as a beach ball, but it's about as big around as somebody's head, an average person. Anyway, what's cool is you can actually send a ball, most people don't know this, you can send a ball in the mail unwrapped, the postal service actually just puts stamps on the ball, and you write the mailing address, the to and from. And the cool thing is, they don't put them in postal boxes, because they don't fit. So the postman, guess what? Has to deliver the ball directly or your AK, your message to your prospector. Whoever you're mailing the ball to. Well these couple stay at home moms came up with this product. You can go to sendaball.com, costs $10. You can mail an actual ball in the mail, but here's what's cool. You type a message on the ball, and these women will paint that message on the ball, and so they'll do it for you. And so, I went ahead and did that. I thought David Frey, David Frey I had already built a relationship with him, but I was like, I'll just be honest with you I thought if I did this I could probably get another endorsement to his list. This would be my second one. Sure, enough I did. He actually called me I was blown away. I sent him a ball and I put, "Have a ball from TwoWeeksNoticeReport.com. It was a website I owned at the time. He was blown away. He couldn't even figure it out he was like, "Wow!" Well he had done a video about it. He started doing a video newsletter and he was talking about his experience with the ball. How the postman, who only comes up when they have packages to deliver that don't fit in the box. And he said, "Hey, here's your package." And it was a green ball. And so he was like, "Hey, this is it?" And all his employees were looking around and everything, and then he noticed it was from David Dutton and he already knew me. And he went to my website and all this stuff. He was blown away. He was like, "Dude, I did not know you could mail a ball." So he does a video about it and puts my web address in there. So, of course, I made sales from that and I built my list. I'm sitting there flipping through one of my favorite magazines which David Frey happens to write an article about called Millionaire Blueprints Magazine. I love that magazine. I'm flipping through, he's doing an article on, I think it was marketing strategies just to get people's attention or something. I'm flipping the pages, looking at the magazine, I see the green ball, and he talks about it. He didn't use David Dutton in the article, but he says, "A friend of his from Tennessee." Which is me, sent him this ball. And he tells the story and I see the actual ball I mailed him in the mail. So, I actually, technically made it to a nationwide, national magazine. And I was talking to Leo Quinn, Leo Quinn was so funny. He was telling me about him sending my ball and I was like, "Where did you learn about that?" He said from David Frey. I said, "You know that guy he was talking about? That's me." So, it's so funny Leo Quinn started using the ball thing because of that. But that's just one way you can get somebody's attention is the bottom line. And plus, it creates fun that Seth Godin talks about. I sent it to a local newspaper in town when I was doing a seminar and I wanted to get people to talk about me, so I sent it to the secretary who loves to talk. She still keeps that ball on her desk and when she's stressed out they'll play with the ball. Guess who is on there? It's me.

BEN SETTLE: Anytime you want a toehold into that newspaper you've got a good contact now.

DAVID DUTTON: Oh, exactly. I'm done. And everybody knows me, why? Because they want to know who sent the ball. So the whole staff knows me, $10. And so if your lifetime value, and that's really cheap, but if your lifetime value of a customer can pay for that, meaning if you make enough off your customer long term, if that person were to become a customer that you sent a ball to, do it.

And you just have a goal, have a plan. I mean, I'm trying to visualize how I'm going to be on the Donny Deutsch show now, and I'm not even close to being on there.

BEN SETTLE: I really appreciate you doing this, because you have shared way more information, I think, than you even intended to share here. And believe me, everyone who's listening to this really appreciates it, too. And I just want to let everyone know that if you would like to get a copy of David's report free just go to: www.mostconnectedmarketer.com and that includes the email he was talking about and basically how he was able to set these deals up. And David did you have something you wanted to give to my subscribers to in addition to that?

DAVID DUTTON: Anybody that knows me knows I'm real big about taking action. Nothing happens until you take action. I want people to not just take this interview and say, "Wow, that's really cool." And just day dream about putting a deal together, I want somebody to put a deal together. Whatever it is that you want to do, but some people lack the confidence just because of the way they're brought up, the way they hung out with people, all these different factors. Sometimes people lack the confidence. That's okay, it's not a problem. For a fee, for a small investment I'm going to help you, I'm almost going to do it for you, help you put your first deal together. I'm just pretty much like, "Hey, do this, do that. When he calls do this." That type of thing. So, anyway that's my special offer I want to give to your subscribers. If they want to put together their first deal I will let them do it with me, personally. This is not a group seminar. This is like me and you on the phone rapping about how we're going to close a joint venture deal, whatever it may be.

You're going to get the most connected man on the Internet for one hour. If you've got something of value I might share it with my contacts. If I like what you're doing and I see that you're passionate about, you're not just trying to make a buck off people. And I don't mind people making a dollar, but you got to love what you do and be passionate about what you're selling. And if you are, I have a lot of contacts that have huge lists. I'm the only person to get four endorsements with David Frey's lists. So I do have the connections to do that.

Chapter 2
Neuroscience Geek Reveals How to Build a Big, Responsive List of Leads Who Already Want to Buy What You're Selling

BEN SETTLE: Ryan, tell us your background.

RYAN LEVESQUE: The quick 30-second version is this. In college, I studied neuroscience and Chinese, and decided to do absolutely nothing with either of those degrees after graduating. After graduating I worked on Wall Street for a few years and then really wanted to find a way to get over to Asia and live the fat cat expat lifestyle for a few years with my wife. I did that, working a corporate gig where I was running a massive sales office expansion project in China, basically flying around the country, living out of hotels and tethered to the Blackberry. It was a cool job, very exciting, sort of wild, wild west, and I got very much burned out. In the meantime, I'd heard about some friends of mine who were making a lot of money doing stuff on "the internet," so I turned on to a few internet marketers and kind of learned the game. Long story short, I started moonlighting as an entrepreneur nights and weekends, and launched a niche info product business that I was able to take from nothing to $20,000 a month in 18 months. At that point I said, "Okay, this stuff works." I quit my job and my wife and I traveled around Asia for a while. Then we moved back to the United States and we're in Texas now. This was back in 2008 and I really haven't looked back since. I've had a few other businesses since then, and this is what I do all day every day.

BEN SETTLE: You grew a business from nothing to $20K per month in less than two years, is that right?

RYAN LEVESQUE: Yeah, in 18 months. People hear that and they're like, "Wow, that's pretty cool," but the real story is there were six months of struggle and heartache and pain that led up to that, where I was really spinning my wheels and not making a lot of progress and doing everything wrong, just part of the growing pains. I think it's an interesting story because it actually ties into some of the psychological conversion-boosting tactics that we'll be talking about on the call, so I'm happy to go into that in a little more detail.

BEN SETTLE: We can, but first let's talk about this whole idea of neuroscience. How has that helped you with marketing, and specifically with getting higher-quality people on your list and converting more of them into buyers?

RYAN LEVESQUE: That's a great question. It's one that we could answer in one sentence, and it's one that we could spend the next hour talking about. In a nutshell, I think the extent to which you can understand how the human brain works and how your prospect's mind works, and not only understand that but leverage that knowledge through persuasion and through using language to influence in an ethical and positive way your prospects, your success – especially as a copywriter, and specifically as an email copywriter – I think largely hinges on that ability.

Whether you have an academic background in a discipline like psychology or neuroscience or cognitive neuroscience, that's really less important I think than having an insane curiosity to learn more about how the human mind works. As someone who has an academic background in neuroscience, I'll tell you the academic piece isn't super-useful. I'm looking at my bookshelf right now and I've got 7 or 8 neuroscience textbooks. Those books collect dust on my shelf, but books like Robert Cialdini's *Influence* and books like *Persuasion* and books that bridge the gap between the academic science of neuroscience and the practical application of it in marketing – I think that's where if you're someone who's a student of marketing, a student of persuasion, a student of copywriting, that's time well spent.

BEN SETTLE: Before we get into these five themes, which I'm very interested in hearing, let's go back to what you were saying before about that business you grew and how it ties into all this.

RYAN LEVESQUE: Sure. I think with a lot of people that maybe are just starting out, the way I approached growing my first business is I had looked towards setting some really high-reach goals. For example, I said I wanted to be making $100,000 in six months out of this part-time business - $100,000 a year net within six months. I would state that affirmation every day and read the little piece of paper in my wallet and think I was doing all these really cool things, and I thought that was the key to making big progress – to kind of sear that in your brain, so you're basically like this automaton zombie that in your sleep you could recite that affirmation. Everything hinged on that – setting the big goal, searing it into your brain, thinking about that big goal 24/7, and doing nothing but taking action towards reaching that big goal. When I had that mindset for six months I was spinning my wheels, but when I turned back to my understanding of human psychology, I realized that the reason why we spin our wheels when we do that sort of thing is because of our brain's natural fear response toward change – whether it's positive change or negative change – and it ultimately comes down to our fight or flight response. When I took a step back and said, "Instead of trying to focus on generating $100,000 a year, why don't I focus on generating one sale in the next 24 hours" – a tiny little goal that I could really break it down and say, "I can do this." It's a small enough goal that your brain says, "This is doable."

$100,000 in six months isn't something that you can really wrap your arms around. There's a lot to making that happen, but getting one sale in 24 hours – you could send an email to all your friends, you could go on forums and go crazy responding to people, offering to answer their questions and upselling them on your product as an info product, you could pick up the phone and call people who are in your niche. There are so many things you could do to generate that one sale. That's the back-story, but when I started shifting my mindset from thinking big to thinking small, that's when all the progress started happening. Ultimately what I did was started thinking in $500 chunks. I said, "What can I do this month that's going to add $500 to my bottom line? Then what can I do next month that's going to add an additional $500?" That $500 for me was a big enough number that it was interesting, but it was small enough that I could actually map it back to specific actions that were doable. It could be sending out an extra email. It could be adding an additional product. It could be reaching out to a few potential JV partners, but it was doable. That's the back-story, and what I want to talk about is the neuroscience behind all that. Why is that approach so effective? Why is it so effective not only in your own life as an entrepreneur or business person, but also why is it effective when you treat your prospects the same way?

BEN SETTLE: That reminds me of this thing from Robert Kiyosaki. I read in one of his books and he was like, "Just make goals that are so small that it's boring, like your goal is to just get up. Just open your computer and turn it on. That's your only goal. You get so bored with it that you keep going further and further."

RYAN LEVESQUE: Right. It's like if you map it back to writing an email, if you're thinking you have to write one of your monthly newsletters. If you were to just sit down and say, "I've got to write this newsletter," it becomes this monkey on your back. You're like, "Shit, what the hell am I going to write about?" and you start getting nervous and all this anxiety builds up. If instead you say, "I'm going to sit down at my computer and I'm going to have the goal of just writing one sentence," you'll say, "I can do that. I can write one sentence." If a sentence is too big, you can shrink that goal even further. You can say, "I can type one word." That's a goal that if you said it to yourself you would say, "Well duh, of course I can do that."

It all has to do with this concept that is actually a term in Japanese business called kaizen. It's the idea that big changes occur not through big actions but through the accumulation of hundreds and thousands of tiny little actions. This idea of kaizen really appealed to me. It was this idea that change doesn't occur all at once, but if you can shrink your goals down to the smallest possible next step that's so small that it's literally impossible for you to fail, that's when I started making all this progress. This is interesting and theoretically this is cool, but there's actually something that's going on in your brain, which is the reason why it's so powerful, and this is the neuroscience angle behind it. You're familiar with the reptilian brain, what we call the higher-thinking brain or the neo-cortex, our ancestors largely operated on our fight or flight response. Any change that occurred would set the warning bells off in our brain, specifically in an area in our brain that's called the amygdala. You don't need to worry about the names, but I'm just giving you the background, so if you're a science junkie you kind of understand that there is something to this. This isn't just hocus-pocus. Our fight or flight response actually resides in this structure in our mid-brain known as the amygdala, and what happens is anytime that your brain perceives any sort of change – whether that's a positive change or a negative change – what happens is your neo-cortex or higher-thinking brain shuts down and your primitive reptilian brain all the sudden takes over. You get into this mode where you get nervous, you get sweaty, you're not sure if it's the right thing to do, you get the butterflies in your stomach, and you basically close off your ability to do any sort of creative problem-solving or do any sort of rational analysis. You're just operating on a very primitive reptilian level. The key to 'hacking your brain' so to speak is to short-circuit that process. The way that you do it is you have to trick your brain into thinking that you're not making any change, or that the change is so small and so imperceptible to your brain that those warning bells never fire off.

Coming back to the business example, the idea of making $100,000 in six months – most people starting from scratch would say, "That's a hell of a great accomplishment," but it's also scary to your brain because it's this idea of change, even though it's positive. But if you can map it back to say finding a dollar bill on the side of the road, that's nothing. That doesn't really change your life in any way, shape, or form, but it's small enough that you could work towards that goal without having that sort of fear response paralyze you. That's sort of the neuroscience behind it so you understand that you can apply it to your own life in terms of the goals that you set for yourself, but more importantly for this conversation you can actually apply it to how you influence your prospects. That's really what I think is going to be most interesting to people listening to this call.

BEN SETTLE: Those are micro-commitments. Is that the layman's term?

RYAN LEVESQUE: Exactly. That's the idea of micro-commitments. We set the stage that making any change is scary. If you think about that in terms of your prospects, their brains don't operate that much differently from your own brain. Any change to them is also scary, so opting in and giving you their email address and their name in exchange for the ability to market to them, or maybe give you their physical address and money in exchange for a product, that's a big change and that's scary. If you can boil that down to a tiny little step that they might take that leads to that big change, all the sudden you're able to bypass that fear response in their brain and you're able to get them into action-taking mode. It's almost like getting someone to dip their toe in water rather than jumping in and doing a cannonball. The idea of micro-commitments is if you can get people to take tiny little steps before the optin process, you can actually dramatically improve your conversion rates because the folks who are either on the fence or maybe aren't quite sure if they're prepared to optin, you can get them to at least dip their toe. By getting them to dip their toe, they're that much more likely to actually opt in when you present them with an optin form. Does that make sense?

BEN SETTLE: Yeah, and it's very interesting. It's just making it easier and more comfortable for them. People get kind of scared. They think they're going to get charged for something if they put their email address in.

RYAN LEVESQUE: Maybe you've done this, and I know I've done it – sometimes when I opt into a list I'm like, "You know what, I don't feel comfortable even entering my real name in this list. I'm going to be Bill. I'm not going to be Ryan, I'm going to be Bill, because I don't know what this guy's going to do with this information," right?

BEN SETTLE: It's true. If I don't see a privacy policy I usually don't. I'll create an email address for a throwaway to sign up on a list, and that email address is getting spam, and yet it's only been used that one time.

RYAN LEVESQUE: I know. People have been burned in the past, so it's a way for them to dip their toe.

This is all great, but it's all very theoretical, so what the hell is a micro-commitment and how can you get someone to take it before they opt in? A micro-commitment can be a number of things, but in the context of this conversation, rather than getting someone to opt in, you can get people to answer a multiple-choice question either framed in the form of a survey, questionnaire, a quiz, or a test of some sort. What it does is it allows them to get into action-taking mode before giving you that precious information. You might say, "Discover 7 ways to boost your bottom line in the next month." Rather than saying, "All you need to do is enter your name and email and I'll give you the information," you might say, "Tell me, which of the following is most important to you right now?" and you have three multiple-choice questions.

They see that and that's it. That's all they see. They don't see an optin form. They see that and they think, "I'm curious to kind of know where this is going, so I'm going to answer this question." Maybe it's, "Growing my email list, improving my online conversion rates, or finding a way to market to my list offline." Maybe in this fictitious example they click the first answer. They say, "I want to grow my list," and they click on that. Then another question pops up and says, "Tell me specifically, how are you driving traffic to your site to grow your list? Primarily through SEO? Paid traffic? Or JV traffic?" and they click SEO.

Then say, "I have a personalized solution for you specifically geared towards folks who are looking to build their list through SEO traffic. If you'd like to get your hands on it, all you need to do is enter your name and email and I'll give you this personalized solution right now." You see what we've done here? We've asked a few questions to get them into this action-taking momentum. You can do this two-step version that we just went through or you could do this through a 5-step version, but the idea is that once they get into that mode you sort of get the momentum going, they're taking these micro-commitments, and they become that much more likely to optin. In Cialdini's framework you can call it consistency and commitment, because they've already expressed that they're interested enough in your solution to go through three or four questions. They've already gone 9/10 of the way, and they're going to go that final 10% and actually get at it, if that makes sense.

BEN SETTLE: Do you find that the quality of the optin is higher this way as well, I would imagine?

RYAN LEVESQUE: It is, so there's all sorts of side benefits to this as well. We were just talking about the fact that this can improve conversion rates. What is also does is allows you to segment your audience. As you know, the more you can segment your audience, the more specifically you can market to them. All the sudden you have somebody who's raised their hand and they've told you two things. They've said, "I'm interested in building my list, and I drive traffic to my site through SEO." So all the sudden you can start putting offers in front of them that are geared specifically to that type of prospect. You can ignore the PPC stuff. You can ignore the JV stuff. You can ignore the conversion stuff because they're still in list building mode. You can focus on two things: driving traffic to their site through SEO and building their list. So not only is it a higher-quality prospect because they've gone through a few hurdles and they've said, "I'm interested enough in this, even after jumping through these hurdles," so yes, you're right. You're going to have less CAN-SPAM flak, because people have raised their hand and said that they're really interested, and you're going to be able to market to them so much more specifically that you're going to be able to better fine-tune your offers or messages to what it is that they want.

BEN SETTLE: That's beyond useful. [laughing] We're going to be testing your plugin probably in the next two or three weeks in a business I partner in. I'm really excited about it because it's been a huge problem. We've been sending everyone to one optin, and you don't know what they're interested in, so we're rotating offers and we're probably boring the hell out of half of them at any given time.

RYAN LEVESQUE: Right. This is perfect for that. I don't want to lose the momentum of the conversation, but I will mention this. Jack and I just released a new version of the plugin. It gives you the ability to create these survey funnels not only using that little tab on the left-hand side like in the demo video, but you can also create them directly in pages and posts and in sidebar widgets as well. For example, maybe you have an ad on your site, or what appears to be an ad. Instead of sending someone to one offer when they click on that ad, you could elicit a simple pop-up survey thing which sends them into the best affiliate offer based on how they answer that question, and you could do the same thing in a page or post as well. We've added a few additional features that I think will give you some more mileage as you're testing this out on your site.

BEN SETTLE: I didn't even really think about the applications for affiliate marketers with this. This is going to make their lives very easy, I would imagine.

RYAN LEVESQUE: Yeah, because a lot of times if you've got a general page it's like, "I've got five different types of people who visit this page. I can't put five different offers. It doesn't really make sense to randomize them on rotation, because it's not so much that one offer converts better than the other, it's the fact that one offer converts better to a certain type of prospect." This bridges that gap. I don't know if you know Howie Jacobsen.

BEN SETTLE: I don't know him personally, but I know who he is.

RYAN LEVESQUE: I was talking to him and I said, "This is sort of like the next evolution in marketing online." If you go back 10 years, maybe six years, people would send all their traffic to their home page. No matter where the traffic was coming from, everything went back to their home page. Then people realized, "Hey, this isn't specific enough, because you've got so many different audiences, so the home page isn't the best place to send people." Then people started creating landing pages. Landing pages were a little bit better tailored. Maybe they'd be keyword-specific, but still there's certain keywords out there, like *lose weight* for example, that tell you almost nothing about who the prospect is. Are they a man? Are they a woman? Are they 65? Are they 25? Are they morbidly obese? Are they 5 pounds overweight? Are they trying to get in shape for an event? Are they trying to lose 50 pounds? It tells you nothing, so people started putting in squeeze pages.

This takes the squeeze page to the next level, because it allows you to insert almost this intermediary step between your end-offer and your landing page that allows you to almost differentiate yourself in any marketplace, because in every marketplace you've got people who are saying, "My solution is the best. We're all things to all people. No matter what your situation may be, we're the ones you should call." This allows you to say, "Time out a second. Before I can tell you whether or not we're the best solution, I need to get to know you a little bit better." In the same way as if you were having a one-on-one conversation with your prospect, you'd ask a few thoughtful questions before you recommended a product to them or recommended a solution. This tool fills that gap. It makes it possible for anybody using WordPress to implement it in just a few mouse clicks, with no programming knowledge needed.

BEN SETTLE: Nice. The next thing I wanted to ask you about was using open loops.

RYAN LEVESQUE: An open loop is just a way to describe it. For example, if you watch a television show and the television show ends on a cliffhanger and they say, "Stay tuned for scenes from next week's episode of The Walking Dead" or Mad Men or whatever it may be, they insert this open loop. The show has planted the seed in your mind and there's no closure in your mind because you want to know what happens next. Television shows do this beautifully. Serial novels do this beautifully.

When you create an open loop, basically what happens is you simultaneously create tension and desire in your prospect's brain, and that is like a lethal combination of neurotransmitters that is like the optimal situation that you want to create in your prospect's brain.

I'll give you an example in a second so this makes sense, but when you plant a seed where you say in your copy, "In today's email we're going to cover the most powerful techniques and most powerful ways to build your list. Oh, before I forget, remind me to tell you that at the end of this email I'm also going to show you how to boost your conversion by 10%, but we'll talk about that later. Okay, moving on…" When you've done that little kind of sidebar note that I just inserted, all the sudden people want to know what that tip or that little technique is. You've introduced that open loop, so that allows you to maintain attention throughout the email because they're waiting for that big payoff at the end of your copy. You can create open loops within open loops and nest them within one another. You constantly want to create this sense that you're never giving 100% closure when you're talking to your prospects.

Mapping that back to the conversation now, sort of the idea of the survey funnel, when you ask people a few questions like the example that we just went through, and you say something like, "To find out the customized solution for folks who are looking to build their list through SEO traffic, all you need to do is enter your name and email," you've created this open loop because they want to know what that semi-customized solution is. They've taken a few steps to describe their situation, and now they want to know, "Now that I've done that, what is this customized solution like?" and you've created this open loop. When you create an open loop like that, it's uncomfortable in your prospect's brain. They have this flood of two neurotransmitters in their brain. One is epinephrine, which is more commonly known as adrenaline, which creates this tension, and the other is dopamine, which is the reward neurotransmitter.

People have this flood and they want to get the reward, they want to get the big payoff that you've teased them with but haven't given to them, and at the same time you've created this tension in their mind. They're saying, "I want to know what this is! I want to know what this is!" When you do that, your prospect's brain is on high alert and they want what you are promising them. What happens at a deep cellular level is you get this release of those two neurotransmitters and it only lasts for a finite period of time. It's like you almost create this chemical reaction in your prospect's brain. It's the coolest thing ever. If you study MRI scans that institutions have done when people are in the middle of a buying decision, you actually can see the neurotransmitters floating around in people's brains. It creates this temporary euphoria where they want to have what you're promising. That's again a very long answer to a short question about how open loops operate from a neuro-scientific angle.

BEN SETTLE: It's fascinating that we're mixing and matching the chemicals in their brain with words. I had no idea.

RYAN LEVESQUE: It's pretty freaking cool. Here's the corollary to this, and this is like theme #3 on our list. You can use open loops to cause the release of dopamine and adrenaline. The catch is that flood of neurotransmitters only lasts for a finite period of time. You get a big spike and it roughly corresponds to about a 20-minute spike. You've got all these chemicals floating around in your prospect's mind and you've got about a 20-minute window to take advantage of it. You elicited that response and it's not going to be there forever. What that means is that in your marketing, whether you're writing a sales letter, an email, or in my case we do a lot of video sales letters, I try whenever possible to keep the sales pitch to a 20-minute length for that reason. That's basically the length of time that you have to keep, maintain, and leverage the attention that you've garnered from your prospect. I don't know if you saw the survey funnel video sales letter. The demo video is under 20 minutes. I think it's between 15-16 minutes, and there's a reason for that, because when people get excited about something you want to strike when the iron's hot. For folks who might be looking at writing sales letters or emails, that's the window that you have. I know webinars are all the rage now, but you don't want something that's going to take an hour and a half to get your message across to your prospect. You want to give them the opportunity to take action while they've got that chemical cocktail in their brain.

BEN SETTLE: That's fascinating. That 20-minute thing makes a lot of sense, too. One of my business partners – I don't know if he understands the dopamine adrenaline neurotransmitter cocktail angle, but he has the same type of rule. He never goes over 18-20 minutes.

RYAN LEVESQUE: That's funny, and there's a reason for that. It's almost like vodka Red Bull. It's a lethal concoction. You've got the Red Bull, which is the stimulant. You've got the vodka, which kind of makes you loose. It's the same thing that's going on in your brain, in a very different way of course, but it's that combination of dopamine and adrenaline which gets them all hot and bothered and wanting what you've got. Strike while the iron's hot in that 20-minute window.

BEN SETTLE: Let's go onto the contrarian optin angle. I've been wanting to hear this all week.

RYAN LEVESQUE: One of the things that I use a lot is almost like what many people in laymen's terms would call reverse psychology, but let's take a step back. In most marketplaces, everyone is raising their hand saying, "7 powerful ways to lose weight.

It's the ultimate weight loss solution. Get access to this solution. All you need to do is enter your name and email." It's like this hard sell to get people to opt into your list. But you can take a step back, and instead of trying to sell people on your solution, you almost take a laid-back approach. You say, "Listen, I've got the best solution out there, but here's the deal. I don't work with everybody. In fact, I only work with a select few number of people. To prove to me that you qualify or you're a good fit for my solution, you need to answer a few questions first. To find out if you qualify, answer the three simple questions that pop up, enter your name and email, and when you've done that I'll let you know if you're a good fit for this solution."

When you do that it almost exudes confidence in your copy that your solution is "the shit," so you're not trying to over-sell yourself and it flips the whole selling angle on its head. It's like putting someone in a job interview. When someone's in a job interview, they're in desperation and they're trying to sell themselves for everything that they've got, and that's basically what you're doing. You're flipping it on its head. All the sudden the prospect's saying, "I need to prove that I'm worthy of this solution." They're no longer wondering if your ethical bribe that they're going to get in exchange for entering their name and email is worth their time. They're thinking, "What's it going to take for me to qualify?" It creates this intellectual problem in their mind once you start asking the questions.

In the fitness market you might say, "For the right person, our supplement is the most powerful on the market. The thing is, this does not work for everybody. In fact, it only works for a select number of people. Answer these three simple questions and I'll be able to tell you right now if you're a good fit." People become curious and they want to know if they're a good fit. You might ask things like, "How would you describe your body type? Are you lean, muscular, flabby? What's your age? What's your gender?" and a few questions like that. You flip the optin thing on its head. You say, "Find out if you qualify for this solution" instead of "Get access now." It's counterintuitive, but in every single test that I've done across markets in the make money space and not make money space, the "Find out if you qualify" angle almost always out-performs.

BEN SETTLE: It's a nice take-away, too. Like you said, people are used to being pitched constantly, and it's a reverse pitch. It's almost like they have to sell themselves on you, mentally.

RYAN LEVESQUE: Right, it does a couple things. You can save people time and save yourself time. If someone genuinely isn't a good fit, you can tell them right off the bat. You can say, "Listen, to be perfectly honest, based on the way you answered those questions I don't think I'm going to be able to help you. However, my buddy Ben down the street has this product that I think is going to be perfect for you." All the sudden it's like, "Holy shit." People believe what you say because you've almost made this damaging admission. You say, "Listen, my product isn't right for you, but I want to be your trusted advisor and I'm going to at least point you in the right direction, so let me tell you about this other thing that may be a better fit for you."

What happens is they've kind of bonded to you because you haven't tried to pitch them. Whether or not they're a good fit, you've taken a step back and you've done more of a consultative assisted sale, so they look at you in a very different way. If someone's not a good fit and you can tell them up front, you don't need to waste time and energy marketing to that person. In the best-case scenario, you can funnel them to something that may be a better fit. Worst-case scenario, you've taken someone out of your marketing system and you might not even want them opting into your list. That way you have a much lower risk of getting spam complaints and wasting your customer service resources on customers that are just going to refund anyway because they're not a good fit for your product. So, there are all sorts of side benefits to taking that angle, in addition to improving your conversion rate.

BEN SETTLE: It seems to me the obvious thing to do if they don't qualify for your product is to send them to an affiliate offer.

RYAN LEVESQUE: Exactly. I know you're in different markets, and I'm sure you think in your markets your solution is good, and maybe it's the best one in the market, but there are other solutions out there. If you have a course for right-handed golfers and someone says they're left-handed, maybe yours isn't the right thing, so you send them to the left-handed golfer's course. They're going to thank you because of that, and everyone is going to end up being better off because you're right. The affiliate offer might be a better-converting offer than your own offer for that segment of your market, and you've kind of nipped the bud up front.

BEN SETTLE: I'm thinking especially for people who use paid traffic, this sort of thing is a no-brainer. This makes it so that you're far more likely to at least break even on whatever you spend.

RYAN LEVESQUE: Yeah, there's so many benefits to this. It's almost like taking a step back. Like many strategies, it's one of these things that if everybody in the marketplace started taking this angle maybe it would lose its effect, but I don't see that happening anytime soon, because people become so enamored and in love with their own solution that they're afraid to do this sort of thing. Really, instead of focusing on their product they should be focusing on their customer, and trying to give the best possible solution to their customer instead of trying to find a way to sell their product. When you shift your mindset like that, all the sudden this contrarian angle no longer feels contrarian. It sort of feels like the right thing to do, or the only thing to do.

BEN SETTLE: You're reminding me of this guy called the greatest negotiator in the world. That's his thing – the most feared negotiator in the world. His name is Jim Camp and that's exactly what he says. He's all about principles versus tactics. It's all about that. You're not trying to tactically just get everybody to do something. They may not even be a good prospect for you, so why would you waste your time? Everybody benefits if you do the right thing. That's good. That's really good. What is this Forer effect?

RYAN LEVESQUE: In some ways, this ties together everything we've talked about so far, and in some ways it's sort of an advanced concept, and I want to make sure that we do a good job of explaining how it works. It's one of these things that's extremely powerful, but like anything in marketing it can be misused.
I look at persuasion not so much as persuasion per se, but it's the ability to inspire someone to take a positive action. For me, just that change in language helps me understand that what I'm doing is actually designed to give people a positive benefit. It's not designed to trick people into giving me their money. It's almost like if you could persuade someone to eat healthier and get in shape, that person's going to be better off. If you frame it in terms of inspiring them to take action in a positive way, it allows you to market to them a little bit more aggressively than you might otherwise, because you don't have this nagging feeling in the back of your mind that what you're doing is unethical or underhanded. What I just said has absolutely nothing to do with the Forer effect. I just want to give that lead-in. The reason I said that is because the Forer effect is one of these things that in the wrong hands you can do great evil with it, so I'm prefacing the conversation with that.

Basically, in a nutshell the Forer effect is this. As human beings, whenever we take anything from a personality test to a survey to opening up a fortune cookie to reading our daily horoscope, our brain has this tendency to want to ascribe the results of that survey, fortune cookie, or horoscope and map it back to our own life. In other words, we find ways when we read our horoscope to justify why it's true. When someone has their fortune told, even if they don't believe in it, we have this kind of nagging thing that goes on in our brain where we want to say, "Well, maybe there's something to that." Even with our daily horoscope we know. I don't know how many billions of people are on the planet today, but we can safely say there are over a million other people on the planet that share your birthday. There's no way in hell that everybody on March 23, if that's your birthday, is going to come into money at the same time. We rationally know that that's not possible, yet there's a small part of our brain that says, "Maybe there's something to it." The same thing happens when we take personality tests. Have you ever taken the Strengths Finder test, by chance?

BEN SETTLE: No. I've taken the Myers-Briggs test. That's the only one I've ever taken.

RYAN LEVESQUE: I'm a big fan of the Strengths Finder. You buy this book that's like $10 on Amazon, and basically you take this 50- or 200-question test – I can't remember how many questions it is – and the answers to those questions help you identify what your strengths are. These are the things that you're good at irrespective of whatever occupation you might fall under. Whether you're a doctor or copywriter, you might have the ability to be a divergent thinker, for example, somebody's who really great at coming up with 50 novel ideas off the top of your head. Or you might be somebody who's really good at focus, with the ability to hunker down on a task, no matter what it may be, and just put everything aside, put blinders on, and really focus in. That's what the Strengths Finder test is. It's a good example to illustrate the Forer effect. The Forer effect is just a term in psychology, named after a psychologist named Dr. Forer, that says that when you take one of these tests you have this tendency to interpret the results and believe them as being true to you. That's all back story to how can you apply that to marketing. If we go back to this survey funnel thing and you ask people a series of multiple-choice questions, and at the end of those multiple-choice questions you say, "Thank you very much for your answers. Based on your responses I actually have a customized solution that is designed for people in your exact situation. To find out what that customized solution is just enter your name and email and I'll tell you all about it," what you've done is you've capitalized on the Forer effect. After people optin, no matter what you put in front of them, even if it's a generic offer and the placebo effect is at play, they're going to believe that the offer they see is customized to their situation. That means they're going to read your offer, they're going to read your sales letter, or they're going to read your copy through the lens that it's specifically designed for them.

In the same way that if someone wrote you a hand-written letter and said in actual handwriting, "Dear Ben, it's so great to catch up with you. I have this really great thing that I want to tell you about," you're going to be reading that letter through the lens that someone took the time to write to you personally and give you their recommendation on something. In reality, there could just be this sweatshop of grannies in Wisconsin that are handwriting these things to thousands of prospects, but you believe that it's specifically to you. When we go back to the whole personality test and survey thing, that's the Forer effect. The net benefit to you as a marketer when you understand that and can use that ethically is it dramatically improves your conversion rates, because when people think a solution is geared to them personally, it's customized to them, they're much more likely to convert.

If I put together a customized package for you versus saying, "I've got three products that I sell: A, B, and C" or I create something that's 100% customized to you, Ben, which one do you think is going to have a higher conversion rate? The one that's geared toward you. You can create that perception in your marketing that what you've done is packaged together a customized solution, and the prospect is going to be much more likely to convert. You can use that Forer effect by building a simple three- to four-question survey in your marketing and integrating it before people optin.

BEN SETTLE: That's interesting. How does all this relate to the survey funnel plugin that you've created?

RYAN LEVESQUE: That's a great question. Everything we've talked about is sort of like the psychology behind a number of different things. You can apply this psychology in a number of different ways in your marketing, but what we've done is we've created this simple little tool. It's a WordPress plugin that allows you to capitalize on all these psychological effects that we talked about.

- Use micro-commitments and getting people to take baby steps before they make the commitment to optin

- Using open loops by planting a seed in your prospect's mind and teasing them with a big benefit before you actually give it to them

- Holding attention by creating this cocktail of neurotransmitters in your prospect's brain

- Using a contrarian optin angle and positioning your offer as a "Find out if you qualify" offer or "Find out if you're a good fit" versus "This is the best offer for you."

- Using the Forer effect

We've created a simple little tool that allows you to capitalize on all those psychological effects at once by building these simple one-click surveys that automatically funnel people into the most appropriate autoresponder sequence, the most appropriate affiliate offer, the most appropriate CPA offer, the most appropriate sales letter, whatever they need, based specifically on the way in which they answer a few simple survey questions.

The cool thing about this plugin is that it's something that you can set up in just fix or six minutes, all within your WordPress backend, with zero programming required and no coding. All you need to do is literally drag and drop, click a few things, and decide which questions you want to ask your prospects.

It's also the type of thing that it helps to see in action. It's one thing to hear us talk about it or read about it in a transcript, but it's something that when you see the demo and see how it works at play, you'll know in just a few minutes if it's something that you can apply in your business.

For anyone listening to this or reading this who might be wondering, "I'd like to learn more," I think the most helpful thing we can do is point them to a demo of it in action, so they can see how it's being used on a real live website right now.

It's the type of thing that when you see it being used in someone else's business, all the sudden the wheels start turning and you start thinking, "How can I apply this in my business?" In the course of a few minutes, if you're like most people and if it's a good fit for you, you'll probably be writing 10-20 ideas on the back of a napkin.

For more info from Ryan, check out:
www.TheFunnelSpecialist.com

Chapter 3
How to Barter Your Way to a Big, Thriving List of Email Subscribers

If you want to quickly build a responsive email list in the next 30 days... especially if you're just starting online and don't have a lot of money, then the following strategy can get the job done.

Here's the story:

Several years ago, I was struggling to build my email list and nothing seemed to work. I wrote hundreds of ezine articles. I tried setting up joint ventures with other list owners. I even added loads of fresh content to my site hoping to attract search engine traffic and leads.

All of these things were helpful.

But they didn't deliver the big "hit" I wanted.

Then one day, I decided to try something completely different. Something that seemed so obvious. Yet hardly anyone was doing it (must less teaching it). And what I did was "trade" writing a half dozen press releases to a marketer I knew (who had a big list) in exchange for plugging my site a set number of times to his list over the course of a month.

Did it work?

Oh yeah!

In fact, it only took a few hours to write the press releases, and every time he plugged my site a new batch of leads came in like clockwork. Before long... my list was up and running with dozens of fresh new responsive subscribers.

The total cost?

A few hours of my time doing something I enjoyed.

And you can do the exact same thing.

You probably have a skill other list owners in your industry want. It could be writing... web design... programming... SEO... editing audio/video... building websites... or just about anything a list owner in your industry can use. And if you simply find these list owners, you can leverage your time and skills to build your list by trading that skill for endorsing your website.

Of course, the "devil" is in the details, isn't it?

How exactly do you find deals like this?

Fortunately, there are all kinds of ways to do it, here are 5 you can start using as early as today:

1. Social Media Networking

Mostly, I think social media is overrated as a marketing tool.

But one thing I do like about it is how easy it is to meet people you wouldn't know otherwise. With FaceBook, for example, you can befriend someone and get to know them (by chatting them up about common interests, responding to their updates, etc). And sometimes that can naturally turn into a valuable contact. That contact may or may not have a list of people who would be interested in your joining your list. But he/she probably WILL know someone who does and can give you an intro.

2. Ask Your Colleagues

Chances are you know other business owners.

And it can't hurt to ask them:

"Hey, I want to build my list and am wanting to trade my XYZ service/product in exchange for other list owners plugging me to their list. Do you know someone who needs an XYX service/product?"

All it takes is one referral like that, and you're off to the races.

3. Forums

You can also go to online forums where list owners in your industry hang out and look for people asking questions you can answer. Don't try to pitch them your offer. Just answer their questions and be helpful. Eventually you will create relationships with people you help. And when the time is right simply make them your offer.

4. Start Small

Don't poo-poo the smaller lists owners!

Someone with a small list is FAR more likely to accept your offer. And after you've helped them, simply ask if they know someone who might be interested in the same deal... and would they mind giving you an intro?

Again, it's simple referral marketing.

And it lets you leverage social proof to the hilt as you work your way up the food chain to bigger list owners.

5. Excel At What You Do

Finally, as the great negotiator Jim Camp says:

**"The more effective people are,
the more we respect them."**

When you're starting out, it's tough getting anyone to take your calls. But as you rack up successes... and as people on the lists you're promoted to see your name... and as word spreads about how groovy you are at what you do... people will eventually start promoting you without you even asking them.

They'll WANT to do it.

It makes them look good to their lists.

Believe it or not, this happens all the time.

And, it can happen for you, too.

All you have to do is start implementing the information in this article.

Chapter 4
How Even Raw Newbies
Can Quickly Build a List
of Subscribers Who Are
Serious, *Qualified*, and *Eager* to Buy

BEN SETTLE: Jack, tell us about your background and what you do and – not to put you too much on the spot here – but what makes you the guy to listen to when it comes to list building?

JACK BORN: It's great to be here and talking with you about list building. As you know, I'm a huge fan of what you teach about your radio talk show model as far as staying top of mind, and I know we're going to talk about that a little bit later.

I've been making a full-time living online since 2001, I was definitely not one of these folks that you hear that's just hitting home runs right out of the gate. I went down a lot of blind alleys and had to figure out a lot of things that seem obvious in hindsight. I was really searching around to try to figure out how to basically not work for the man. That was the driving force. "How do I not work for the man?" but for a while I did work for the man in a big way. I worked for Merrill Lynch as a financial advisor. I left that after three years. I was doing pretty well, but I joined a start-up company in Jacksonville. I live in Florida. After working for that company for one year, my boss at the time and I both came to the same conclusion at the same time that I was not a good fit for this organization, and probably not a good fit for anywhere in corporate America. I left on my own, and I bought a $70 piece of software actually on the black market, and I created a website that basically did the same function that my ex-boss's company did, with a slightly different twist on it. I spent a year building it up and finally launched it. I did almost everything wrong, but in the process I learned programming and that website went on to pay my mortgage and my lifestyle for about the next five years.

Then I started building websites. I started creating software because I realized I was good at it. I started selling it and I started recruiting affiliates. Then I started to dabble in affiliate marketing itself, selling as an affiliate. I did that pretty effectively. I was very good at doing pre-sells, which we might talk about, but this led to a really important watershed moment in my life. Perry Marshall, the guy who figured out Google AdWords and wrote books and training courses on it and has really been a thought leader in how to buy advertising online, sent out an email to his list, and I was one of the people who received it. He said, "I'm doing a competition. I'm looking to hire an affiliate manager," and this other thing that he called a Content Czar, which was really repurposing content. I had no interest in the Content Czar thing, but I thought, "Man, even though I didn't wake up this morning looking for something – I'm doing fine, I've got some things figured out, I've got my businesses – still, this would be an amazing opportunity. I respect Perry and I just think this would be an amazing opportunity for growth," so I went after it with all my heart and soul and I won. So, for the past 3-1/2 years now I've also been Perry Marshall's marketing manager, just absorbing everything that I can and meeting as many people as I can.

So that's the short-ish version of my background and why someone should listen to me about list building.

BEN SETTLE: I can only think of a handful of people – and maybe I just don't know that many – but I can only think of a handful who are both programmers and marketers anymore. Do you still do those marketing management for Perry Marshall?

JACK BORN: Yeah, I do. Most of it is building out funnels and campaigns. A lot of it is strategic stuff. For example, one of the things that I'm building up this year is taking a program that we did last year for consultants and turning that into an automated funnel and probably adding some new content.

BEN SETTLE: In all the years you've been doing this since 2001, and all of your own companies and then working with Perry Marshall's company and all that, what are some of the big mistakes people are making when building their list, where if they just stopped doing that they would see some pretty good results?

JACK BORN: I'd love to hear what some of your ideas are too, but one of the mistakes that I see people making is really trying to go for volume. In other words, they're just trying to build up their list as big as possible. Of course, having a large tribe or a large audience of folks that pay attention to you is extremely powerful, but what I'm referring to is trying to increase those numbers as fast as possible, with little or no concern for the relationship with that audience, and also the attention that they give you. You and I recently did an interview where I was interviewing you, and it was a fantastic interview. One of my big take-aways was the way in which you use your radio show model to stay top of mind. It's not a matter of, "Okay, I've got you on my list and I'm going to send you the email once a month or even once a week." You do it all the time – if not daily, almost daily – so that's the way that you maintain your relationship. Also, folks who decide, "Ben Settle's way of doing things is not for me. I don't like his voice. I don't like his character. He said something that made me mad," you know what, they get off and they get off early. So, you're basically forcing people to decide. "You're either in this tribe that I'm building or you're not. If you're not, that's fine, but I'm going to have this conversation with my folks every single day, so if you're enjoying this, stay in. If not, here's the button. Get out." I think it's extremely powerful for folks to understand that it's not just the size of your list. Let me just give an example. An example, without naming names, is that one of the things I've done is I've helped get joint venture partners for Perry Marshall. Sometimes you'll have someone with a relatively large list and then someone who has a list that's maybe only one-third or one-fourth the size of the other partner. The interesting thing is that you can send out the same emails that send people to the same landing page, and those two partners do the exact same thing, and you get two completely different results. It's not uncommon for the person with the smaller list to generate far more sales. It doesn't always work out that way, but my point is that it depends on a lot of things. So that's one of the big things, going for size and not staying top of mind. It's about getting their attention and keeping their attention. I've got another mistake that people make, but is there anything that you want to chime in about on some of those ideas?

BEN SETTLE: Yeah. I used to subscribe to Dan Kennedy's newsletter. Last February there was one article in there written by Ryan Deiss. A lot of people are big fans of his. Some people hate him, some people love him, it really doesn't matter. He wrote this article about a splash squeeze page. If you go to whitehouse.org it's like you can sign up for the mailing list or you can bypass it and click to get inside for whatever content, so you give them the option. When I did that, my optins went up like crazy. I had somebody create me one. They're not hard to do. They're pretty simple. The funny thing is, it's been around since like 2000. This concept is not new. My point is, I was getting ready to send Google AdWords traffic to my site. I decided not to do that, for reasons which I won't bore people with right now because it's not important, but in doing that, the guy who was helping me out was Jim Yaghi. Jim was telling me, "Look, you want to put a little checkbox on this so they have to check a box before they can opt in, and under that box it's very blatantly clear with them that they're not only going to get daily emails," which I've already been telling people that, "but they're going to get promotional offers" – all this stuff that most people would be scared to put on there. But what's happened is my optins have not gone down at all since doing that, and the quality of people – just going by what I've been seeing so far – seems to be going up. These are people who are thinking, in most cases. Not everyone does, but these are thinking people. They're better people. They're more likely to buy or at least consider what I have. They're not complainers. They're getting something from the content and they're appreciative of it and they're not really whining about it. I'm just thinking, like you were saying, it's better to have a small list of people like that than a large list of people who are going to make your life a living hell.

JACK BORN: Absolutely. I would say another mistake that people make, particularly online, is not paying attention to the economics. In other words, it's being able and willing to buy media or to pay joint venture partners appropriately to be able to build your list. For example, I was recently having a conversation with someone who specializes in offline marketing. In the offline marketing, it's very common for a marketer to "go negative" on the front end. What that means is that you lost money on the first offer. You send out the direct mail pieces, whether it's to your list, someone else's list, or a totally cold list, and you might lose money on that first offer, but you already have planned in what is going to be on the back-end. What comes next? Are they buying a $100 upsell? Is there a $5,000 course? It could be anything in-between, but the point is that a lot of online marketers are hyper-focused on, "If I'm not making money on that first transaction, then I don't want to do it." A thought experiment that I'd like to pose to people is to think about what would your business have to look like in order for you to lose money on the first sale, and you still are laughing all the way to the bank? What would your business have to look like? How would the economics have to change? What would your follow-up systems with email have to be? What sort of price points would you have to have for the back-end systems? Let's say you're selling a $49 front-end product. If currently all of your marketing is built around, "I can only advertise or only work with partners where I'm making money on that first transaction," it would completely transform your business and allow you to grow your list much, much faster if you were able to go out and actually lose money while building your list, because you know from the economics, because you've been tracking, that you have follow-up offers that come into play, so you get that money back relatively quickly. Does that make sense?

BEN SETTLE: I'm just wondering, are you specifically referring to paid advertising and doing the numbers with that, to send people to your sign-up page and having the economics of that figured out? A lot of people only rely on free traffic.

JACK BORN: That's right. A lot of people only rely on free traffic, and that's mostly what I'm talking about. But let's say if you went to a joint venture partner. If you're completely unknown, if you have the ability to say, "Look, I'm going to give you 100% of the first sale," but you knew you were still going to make plenty of money on the back-end because you've already got your funnel set up, you've tested it and you know that X number of people that buy your front-end product buy the back-end product, it just completely revolutionizes what you're able to do. Folks that might not have decided to do the joint venture relationship with you initially might be open if you're able to basically pay them double. You're paying them 100%. I'm not a huge believer in the concept of free traffic. I know what everyone means, and I'm doing air quotes when I say, "free traffic." I know what everyone means when they say free traffic, and I'm not an SEO expert, but let's face it, SEO takes time. If you're doing social media, if you're putting out a whole bunch of videos, that's extremely valuable. There's a lot of good reasons why you should do it, but it takes your time. The folks that are really doing well with both SEO and with video marketing or article marketing have a team of folks that they're paying so that they can do other things. They've got the system down and they're churning out the videos and their team is putting them up on YouTube, getting them transcribed, etc, so that's another way to look at paid marketing. You have your funnel, so how are you going to get people to your website? Are you going to wait around until someone stumbles into it, or are you going to seize the day and basically write the check to be able to bring people to your funnel? If you don't have a ton of money to start out with, then you've got to bootstrap your way to the point that you can do it. The ability to outsource either the manual labor required to get that social media, videos, and articles out there, or to just straight-out buy the traffic from Facebook, Google, CPV or other places you can buy traffic is extremely powerful, and a lot of people overlook it when it comes to building a list, especially online.

I'll give you another example. One of the people that I've been able to meet recently is the lead marketer for a product called the Pimsleur Approach. The name of the company is different. The Pimsleur Approach is a language learning product. If you haven't heard of that, you've probably heard of Rosetta Stone. Rosetta Stone is a public company, and they love the fact that Rosetta Stone is public because public companies have to talk very publicly and openly. "All right, investors, here's what worked, here's what didn't work. We have all these kiosks and it didn't make money, but here's what we're planning on doing next year." Not only do they basically have to share everything that they did last year, but they talk about their plans going forward, so it's beautiful for them. The Pimsleur Approach folks drive a lot of traffic through a lot of different resources, but one of their main sources of traffic are called CPA networks. I don't want to get too far down this rabbit hole, but basically these are affiliates that can send massive amounts of traffic – server-melting types of traffic – but they're looking at the numbers. For them it's not who you know, it's not this buddy-buddy deal, it's just purely on the numbers. It's just purely a money play. When they look at the numbers, basically for every 1,000 emails that go out, based on these numbers how much money should I be expected to bring in, and should I send out this guy's email or this guy's email? The Pimsleur Approach folks have set up their metrics where they've got a continuity program, and their conversion rates are so high and their stick rate is such that a lot of times they will pay out the affiliate twice what they made on the first sale, and they're still making money. The affiliates end up mailing over and over and over because it's a very profitable campaign. That's the point. They're able to grow this massive list because they're not trying to make money on that first sale. They know that the money will come, because they set it up that way. They're not doing it based on faith, they know because they've tested their stuff and they're continuously split testing to make sure that their funnel is producing as much revenue as possible.

BEN SETTLE: I used to have this client in the self-defense niche, back when I did client work, and he approaches this very similar I think to what you're saying. He's done the numbers and he no longer even creates a free optin list. He doesn't have that. He sends paid traffic to a $70-80 product, and this works for him I think because he's in a mass market type thing.

He'll get like 10,000 visitors a day, and all he wants is a sale. If you don't buy, he's not going to talk to you ever again on his list. All he wants is that list of buyers, because he's done the math and I'm assuming he breaks even or maybe only loses a little bit, but then he has his back-end in place to pick up the slack, where everybody is segmented out and all that.

JACK BORN: That's very powerful. I've seen other people do that as well. Again, along the lines of being curious and always wanting to try new stuff, one of the things that I'm going to be testing with a funnel that I'm setting up for Perry Marshall's business is the option to optin for a donation. That really kind of works hand-in-hand with who Perry is. If you don't know Perry, he's big into certain causes, so the idea is you can't get on the list for free, but if you want to make a donation, here's a couple charities that you can choose and donate to. There's some reasons why that's important, but one of them is that, just as you were talking about before, when someone does that, we're going to make sure that they're understanding, "You're going to get an email every single day for the next 30 days and here's what you're going to learn." Now they're expecting it, so now they know to look for it. Plus, even though it was a donation, they paid for it so now it's even more valuable. Now it's even more top of mind. So they know what to expect and it's also very, very top of mind because they pulled out their credit card and paid something, or they typed in their PayPal information and paid something. The final thing – and this is a little bit tricky – but the way that we're doing the donation, we're going to actually be able to gather their direct mail address when they make the donation, even though the donation goes directly to someone else. We'll be able to capture that information and we're going to send out direct mail to them as well. That's something that we're trying. The concept of going for a smaller sale but forcing someone to make a purchase before they get on your list is very, very powerful. It's called buying momentum. Once someone makes a purchase, now the decision has gone from, "Should I buy or should I not buy?" to "How much should I buy?" and that's a really important distinction.

BEN SETTLE: That's really good information. That's awesome. Last year I interviewed you and Ryan Levesque and we got deep. I'm not saying we have to get that deep, but we got deep into the psychology of list building. I was wondering if you could share some tips you've learned through your years of doing all this, on the psychological aspect, just a shift in understanding buying behavior and that sort of thing, and how to build a list.

JACK BORN: Sure. One of the most effective techniques that I've employed we already discussed when we had that interview with Ryan, but it's worth repeating again. That's this concept of involvement. A lot of squeeze pages, optin pages, or lead pages, when the visitor arrives there they're just presented with some bullets, a headline, and name and email and that's it. Right off the bat you're asking for something and you're not invoking any sort of curiosity, so you're not switching them from browsing mode to getting involved. You want some sort of involvement device. Again, this is borrowed somewhat from the offline world. A lot of very successful direct mail pieces involve the seemingly-silly involvement pieces where you're supposed to take the sticker and peel it off and put it on the prize that you won. Why do they have you do that? It's to get you involved. If they get you involved, you're more likely to send it back or call in or whatever it is that they want you to do, whatever the call to action is. Let's walk this through and talk about how this would work in the online world. How do you use an involvement device? It's very, very simple and extremely effective. It's a lot easier than doing it offline.

Let's say that we were advertising to the golfing market. Instead of saying, "We have an ebook that we want to provide to you. Just give us your name and email and we'll send it right out to you," wouldn't it be more interesting to ask someone, "We have some very valuable information. Before we send that to you, we want to ask you just a few questions to make sure that we send you the right information. First of all, do you hook or do you slice? Which is the biggest problem that you have with your golf game?" Anyone who has played golf knows that those are the two main issues that people have. You either hook or you slice. Rarely do you do both. If you do both then you're in loads of trouble, but typically, based on your swing, you're either slicing the ball or hooking the ball. Here's the thing. People who hook the ball think that their problem is uniquely different than the people who slice the ball. People who slice the ball think that their problem and the fix associated with it is uniquely different than the people who hook the ball. Whether that's true or not, that's what they believe. "My deal is different. My situation is different," so why fight that? Ask them, before you even ask for their name and email, "Do you hook the ball or do you slice the ball?" and then they answer that question. The next question could be, "What do you typically score? Are you under 80, do you score above 80 but less than 95, or are you shooting above 95?" You could ask two or three questions and then say, "Great. We have some information for you because you shoot over 95 and you want to shave 5 strokes off your game and you hook the ball. Just put in your name and email and we'll send out some information to you right away that's going to help with your game." What's happened is a couple of things that are very, very powerful.

Ryan and I used to sell a product that made it very easy for folks to do this, but we can talk about some ways to do the low-tech version of this. What it does is that it stops someone from just casually browsing from page to page and gets them involved and that's what you want. Now they're involved with what turns out to be an optin form. They answer the questions and now their curiosity kicks in. They've started a process that is going to drive them crazy to a certain degree if they don't finish it. Certainly, a lot more curiosity has been built up than say three blind bullets plus name and email on your typical squeeze page. Now they're involved and curious. They want to know where this "choose your own adventure" is going to end. When you present them with the name and email, it's a lot more likely that they're going to put in their information. Ryan and I have seen easy double digit increases in conversion rates just by going through this process. It seems counterintuitive because you're putting up some barriers before you're asking for their name and email. You're delaying asking for the name and email by a few clicks, but by getting someone involved, they have to now finish this process in order for them to sort of see where this goes. It's an itch that they now need to scratch, so they enter in their name and email and you take them to the landing page and deliver the information. The other very, very powerful thing about this is that right off the bat you can start to segment your list. That means you can basically group people or tag folks inside of your list with different characteristics. You could have 50% of your list that's indicated that they hook the ball and 50% has indicated that they slice the ball. Then you've got all the other questions. This is very, very powerful because, first of all, you can speak to these different audiences with very specific messages. You could have an autoresponder series that goes to the folks that slice the ball that talks about the problems that you had slicing, maybe a case study of someone who was slicing the ball every single time they went out and stepped up to the tee box, but you were able to fix their slice. Slice, slice, slice, slice. You're not talking about the hook because they don't care about the hook. They don't have the problem of dealing with the hook. That's one very effective thing. Another thing is that you can tailor your products based on certain market segments. You might find out that the folks that hook the ball really aren't that interested in buying products, but the people that slice the ball have their credit card out and they're ready to buy whatever you put in front of them. You definitely want to be watching that so that you can tailor products to your audience. Does that make sense?

BEN SETTLE: It does. That's something I've not tried yet, but I'm keen on trying it because from a certain standpoint it makes a lot of sense. I was thinking of asking questions, not necessarily what their problem is, but "What topic or problem did you buy your last product on? What was that product?" "Well, I bought this product on how to hit the ball farther," which says more about what they're more willing to buy, not necessarily what they think they want to buy, you know what I mean? I don't know how exactly to word that, but it would be good information to have.

JACK BORN: One great way to do it is to survey your list. This doesn't have to do so much with list building, but it would be very powerful to survey your list. Let's say that you're thinking about coming out with a course on search engine optimization. I know that's probably far afield of what you actually would come out with, but let's just pretend. So you wanted to know has your list bought other courses on search engine optimization. Again, this is counterintuitive. If somebody has already bought a course on search engine optimization, someone who doesn't understand psychology would think, "Oh, they probably don't need another one." That's wrong. They probably want to buy another one and another one, so you would want to survey them and say, "Have you ever bought a course on search engine optimization?" If they say yes, then you would want to ask them, "What was the price point?" You'd probably do an open-ended text box of, "What did you like about it?" Another question that you might want to ask would be, "Was this delivered online or was it books and CDs and DVDs or a combination of the two?" From that information, you can start to get an idea of what their buying habits are. I don't know if you've talked to folks who have expressed this, but I know I've talked to a lot of people who are very, very opinionated about how they want to consume content. A lot of folks will say, "I only buy stuff where I can download the MP3s, load them onto my iPod, and listen to them at 1.5X speed so I can get through it very, very quickly. I won't sit there and watch a webinar or watch a video." Other folks are the complete opposite, so that's another thing to think about if you're creating a course. What sort of media is your market's ideal way to consume information?

BEN SETTLE: Sometimes you can do what I've done and do the opposite of what they said. [laughing] You'd be surprised. The way I look at it – and this kind of is related to list building – you probably want to build a list ideally of people that you want to deal with. It doesn't have to be necessarily format, but in any sense, you want to talk about this. I like dealing with people who are readers more than people who are video watchers, not because I think there's anything wrong with people who watch videos, but I just think along the same way and we both consume information and interpret information very similarly. That's just something to think about when you're building a list or selling a product. Who do you want to deal with? I'd rather have a quality person – quality in the sense that they're going to want what I have – versus someone who's going to be fighting me and, "Oh, can you please change your entire business model for me?"

JACK BORN: Absolutely. You'll get those emails in your support desk. I think you make a great point, which is you shouldn't necessarily let the inmates run the asylum, another Dan Kennedy phrase I picked up.

BEN SETTLE: When you do that, at least this has been my experience – I can't say this is everyone's experience – but when they do leave, they don't leave by pushing the Spam button. They're just like, "You know what? I'm just going to unsubscribe." They're not angry at you. You've essentially saved them time. I don't get very many spam complaints, knock on wood. It all comes back to respecting your potential customer. Even if they don't want what you have, you give them that option to leave and let them go. It's a good thing. You had mentioned something earlier when we were talking about segmenting lists. Let's get more into that. You did talk about what it is, but can you repeat what that means just so everyone is crystal clear, because this is what the whole direct mail industry is built on.

JACK BORN: As you mentioned, this is really, really important. If you've never heard of this concept, this is critical to your future success. As you start to bring people into your world, they opt in to receive your free emails if you're using that model, as most people do. You want to start to identify what sort of groups they belong to. Segmenting your list is really just thinking up what different sorts of groups there are that would be useful for you to know. This is just a few examples, but some examples would be where they are, so demographics. Knowing where someone is in the country or in the world is extremely important. We can get back to that in a little bit. Next is who they are. This is incredibly important. I was recently taken aside at a live event this past weekend where I was speaking on a topic, and the event organizer was asking for some help. What it came down to was I said, "You really need to do a much better job of list segmentation, because you're bringing people into your world and you're sending out emails on a regular basis where a lot of these emails have to do with how to be an affiliate. There's a significant portion of the folks on your list who either don't know what affiliate marketing is, so they think 'This is not the right place for me,' or they know what affiliate marketing and they really don't like it. It's just an unappealing thing to them, which is fine." Let's take that example. What I advised that person to do was to use different mechanisms to segment their list. What happens is when he sits down to write an email about affiliate marketing – whether there's an article or a video, he's promoting something, his own product or someone else's product on how to be a better affiliate, how to make more money as an affiliate – he doesn't send this out to his entire list. Now he sends it just to the folks who have self-identified as being interested in affiliate marketing. This is really, really powerful because the folks who are not interested in that topic are never going to see that email. They'll never see that email, and he can send emails that relate to their business model. If they're in the content creation model or creating products or whatever it is that they're doing, he can send offers and content based on what they're interested in. That's the concept behind list segmentation. We talked briefly about where they are in the world. By the way, this is a big one in the offline world, being able to basically eliminate certain areas of the country or the world where you don't want to send direct mail because, unlike email, every time you send out a direct mail piece it has a significant cost to it. If you can eliminate 75% of your direct mail cost, that goes a long way towards turning a money-losing campaign into a profitable campaign. So, where they are can be important, and who they are.

Next is their behavior. Their behavior is really, really important. I think we're going to get into this a little bit later, but in the offline world it would be something like this. If you had a customer that was buying from you every single Christmas, and they buy $5,000 of stuff every single Christmas holiday, when Christmas rolls around you would want to spend a lot more attention with that person. That's a very simple example. Another example would be if you had a jewelry store and you had a bunch of people walk in the store and you didn't have enough staff to be able to talk to all the people walking in the store, you would want to use your vision to be able to see that this one woman over here has six other shopping bags from some other very high-end stores. She's got lots of jewelry. She's got some very expensive sunglasses on and very expensive shoes.

Of all the people in the store, just based on what you can observe about her behavior, you would do well to spend a lot more attention with her than say someone who comes in in cutoff shorts and tennis shoes. It's just a lot more likely that she's there to actually make a purchase. Tracking someone's behavior is really important for lots of reasons, but one of them is if you watch what people do and not listen to what they say, you can pick up some very important data about how to best change your marketing to increase your ROI. Then one that we've touched on before is their interests. What are they interested in? If they're interested in affiliate marketing, great. They may go into the bucket of folks who are interested in affiliate marketing. If they're interested in product creation, then make sure that they're tagged as being interested in product creation. If they're fascinated by mobile marketing and Kindle, then tag them such that when you have a product on that or you're going to promote someone else's product, you don't have to tell your entire list. You can have a very focused conversation with the folks that you know through their behavior are interested in that topic. Is that a good rundown of segmentation?

BEN SETTLE: Yeah. We brought up golf, but this can go for any market. With dog training, you've got different breeds. There's so many ways you can slice and dice a list and segment people out into their own list so that if you have a special offer just on that one problem they're trying to solve, the rest of your list doesn't really care about it. When I'm doing these special sales, I have a copywriting list that's just people interested in copywriting, and I'll do a sale for a copywriting product to my main list, but I'll especially be aggressive with that copywriting list and I can get away with it.

JACK BORN: Absolutely. They've told you that they're interested in that topic, so they don't mind receiving an email every single day. That's what they're interested in. Going back to the dog training just as a quick example, this goes back to everybody thinks that their deal is different. A lot of dog owners think that their dog is completely different, their breed is completely different. They also believe that the problem that their dog is having is completely different. If my dog is barking all the time, certainly a book that deals with just how my breed can stop the barking, I'm going to be a lot more receptive to that. Your product may be a book and training course on how to fix all sorts of behavior problems for dogs, but you're going to have a lot higher response if you're able to segment out your messages in such a way that at least the big segments of your list are getting more personalized messages about how to stop this behavior and that behavior, rather than "I've got a one-size-fits-all solution that just works for everyone." People are just automatically set up to believe that their situation is unique.

BEN SETTLE: You were bringing up the dog stuff and things that are unique. I remember once talking to Terry Dean. We were on some kind of call together. We were both consulting the same client at the same time, and I said something off-hand because I'm ignorant on the subject of running. That's not something I do, but he's a runner. I said, "Aren't all these shoes really the same, just because they say running?" He's like, "No, they're not. Runners have a very specific set of problems they have compared to someone who's hiking or walking." This segmenting is not only important for sales, but for really serving your customer.

JACK BORN: Absolutely. There are both perceived and real differences inside of your market. Certainly
there are a lot more perceived differences than there are real differences, but a lot of your market is looking for a substantially different type of product. If you've got the type of market like dog training where there's, if not hundreds, then dozens of different breeds and many different problems, I'm not suggesting that you put everyone into their own individual group so that you're sending out specific messages to every single person. What's going to happen is that there's going to be some way to 80/20 your list. What I mean by 80/20 is it's using Pareto's 80/20 principle to say, "As I start to segment my list, what segments are showing up that are over-represented?" You might find out there's a ton of people with Labradors. "40% of my list has Labradors, and they have a shedding problem." I'm just totally making this up. I don't think you can fix that with behavior, but the idea would be that you would then focus your resources and energy towards creating a detailed follow-up series of emails to that segment of your list, because it's over-represented.

BEN SETTLE: This is interesting stuff. We're getting into the nitty-gritty here, but I just kind of want to bottom-line it for the person reading this, because what they want to know is, "How am I going to make money off this?" When you've done this, have you seen a huge increase in sales overall when you do this? Even though it might sound counterintuitive that you're actually contacting less people maybe, have you seen a bigger response?

JACK BORN: Absolutely. It's difficult to put a number on exactly what the difference is, because it's very much like a conversation about split testing. In a conversation about split testing, if you were to say, "Does it work? Is it really worth my time to do split testing say on my landing page?" the answer is, "Overwhelmingly yes. It absolutely works. How much money it's going to make you kind of depends on many different factors. It depends on what you're testing. It depends on how good you are at setting up different types of persuasive copy, the layout of your page, it depends on a lot of different things." If someone were just take the concept of, "I'm going to apply split testing and make a lot of money with this," and they start testing minor things like font changes and the color of the background of their website, they may come away from it thinking, "You know what? That really wasn't worth my time at all. I don't know why everyone says split testing is so wonderful." In the same way, segmenting your list can bring you 2X profits or 3X profits. It's not unusual for that to happen. It usually doesn't happen all at once. It's something that you build into, the same way that you build into split testing. You split test one thing, you improve that, then you split test another thing, then you build on that. With list segmentation, it's more along the lines of you focus on one segment of your list, you build out that series or focus your attention on that group, then you say, "What's the next biggest segment of my list, and how should I write my emails to really cater to them?"

BEN SETTLE: When you talk about this, I've heard this before. It's not really an objection, it's more like people are lazy and they don't want to have to do all this work. They'll be like, "So I have to write all these emails for every segment?" I always tell people what I do myself is, "No, because if you're writing emails regularly to your list," at least the way I'm teaching people to do it, "you should have a year's worth of emails eventually anyway, and you can just pick out the ones that are on that topic and just put those in the autoresponder for that segment."

JACK BORN: Absolutely. It might be as simple as looking at the emails that you're sending out and just simply removing the ones that don't apply to them. For example, if you're speaking about several different online marketing topics and you realize that there's a segment of your list that's not interested in affiliate marketing, you might copy the list over and you just remove the ones that talk about affiliate marketing. It could just be that simple. This doesn't have to be complicated. Like I said, you want to start with what you think is going to give you the biggest bang for your buck or your time, so to speak. You want to focus in on, "What are the two or three main segments of my list?" Just by doing that, it's going to be a huge step forward over and above just sending the same emails to everyone and treating everyone the same, because they're not the same and they don't believe that they're the same. If they don't believe they're the same, the old copywriting adage is you want to enter the conversation that's already going on in their mind. Here's the conversation going on in their mind.

"My situation is different. My deal is different. A one-size solution is not going to work for me."

BEN SETTLE: You also just reminded me of something. People can take anything they've already written and just repurpose it for each segment. It could be the same email in every segment, but just a different URL and slightly different call to action.

JACK BORN: Yeah, this doesn't have to be writing your entire email series completely over. Using your radio show method, it's not writing three separate different emails for your three segments every single time. What you could do is, as you mentioned, repurpose the email and just change possibly the opener and how you close out the email. This doesn't have to be a tremendous amount of extra work, but what I would say is, just like split testing, test it out. Go with what you think is going to give you the most bang for your time and test it out. If it works for you, then continue on with it. Take it even further and take it even further, just like you would do with split testing.

BEN SETTLE: What we're doing with this other company that I partner in is we're going to be using your methods and your software and all this. We'll be segmenting buyers of a specific product, because after that we're not really sure what to sell them. We have to figure that out. All I did was I found a copywriter, someone I trust and know and I know he does a really good job, and I just said, "Look, you write these follow-ups and you get 20% of the sales that come from them." Copy is about 20% of the process so it seemed fair to everybody, so you don't have to write your own emails. You can joint venture with someone to do it for you and pay them that way.

JACK BORN: I will mention this. This gets really nitty gritty, but as you were talking about this I thought this would be useful to bring up. I don't do a whole lot on Clickbank anymore, but they're a great platform. If you've never used them I would encourage you to check them out. One reason why you might want to consider selling a product on Clickbank if you were going to pay someone a royalty, say like a copywriter or a programmer, is that Clickbank has something really unique called JV contracts. It's not what you think, because when someone says a JV contract to me, that seems to mean you're going to do a joint venture with someone and they're going to promote your product and you guys decided to write a contract. That's not what this is about at all. What Clickbank will do is they will use their automated processing system to be able to pay say this copywriter 20% of the sales that come in, so imagine this. You go to the copywriter and say, "I'll pay you a 20% royalty on all the sales that come in." Even if the copywriter knows you, probably in the back of their mind they're thinking, "This sounds good, but how long am I going to have to wait before the check gets cut? Is he going to send it in the mail? Is it going to be on time every time? What if he goes on vacation?" The nice thing is with Clickbank, they will automatically split that out, so you're getting the 80% that's left over. Basically, they're paying everyone as they should, and they take another slice off the top that goes to the copywriter, which just makes it really easy if you just want to set it up in an automated fashion and you don't want to have to deal with the payments.

BEN SETTLE: And nobody has to worry about not getting paid, because it's all done through Clickbank.

JACK BORN: Absolutely. According to their marketing literature, and I do believe this, they've never been late with a payment ever. They are 100% on time all the time.

BEN SETTLE: Great. Now let's segue into the next question that I would have and I think a lot of people would have. I'm about as far as you can get from being a techie. I'm lucky I can log into Aweber and send an email every day. That's the extent of my skills. Let's just assume that most of the people reading this are the same way. How can they start segmenting their list, like someone at my level who knows just enough to log into the autoresponder and send an email? That's like the extent of their skills.

JACK BORN: That's a great question. One simple way, regardless of which platform you're using, would be to set up multiple optin pages. I'm giving you the low-tech version, but here it is. You set up multiple optin pages, and on the landing page you could use an involvement piece that could be as simple as, using our golf example, "Do you hook the ball or do you slice the ball?" and those could be hyperlinks. "Do you hook the ball? Click here. Do you slice the ball? Click here." When they click that link, it either takes them to the landing page for folks who hook the ball or it takes them to the landing page for folks that slice the ball. On those two different landing pages you would have set up two different lists. They both end up as subscribers, but one would add them to the list for people who hook the ball and one would add them to the list for people that slice the call. As we've already talked about, you might have 20 follow-up autoresponder emails, and you don't have to write 20 new ones for each list. You can repurpose them, so you might only have to change 10-20% of what you put in there. It really just kind of depends on your market and your product, but in a lot of cases the differences between one list and the other can be mostly cosmetic. Some of it is actually substantive. So that would be the low-tech version of how you could do that. If you wanted to make it even a little bit more advanced, you could take them to a second page that just branches further. If you think of branches on a tree, you could take them to another page that says, "Do you shoot below 80, above 80, or above 90?" and each of those take them to a link, so now you have more pages that they land on. This is really what Ryan and I used to sell in a more packaged format with a WordPress plugin called Survey Funnel. We no longer sell that product. What that did was essentially that function right there that I just explained, but instead of sending people to different pages, it was a light box that would come up on your screen. It was easy to set up because you could use WordPress. That's another way if you're using WordPress that you can start to segment your list.

BEN SETTLE: I'm on Perry Marshall's list, like probably most of the people reading this, and if they're not, they should be on Perry's list. A few months ago he was talking about this tool that you created called AW Pro Tools. What is this? I'm going to be using it, but I have not researched it to the point where I know everything about it. Tell us all about it, because I'm very interested in this and I've not yet asked you about this yet, in this much detail.

JACK BORN: AW Pro Tools is a software platform that's for anyone who uses Aweber. The reason why I chose Aweber is because they currently don't have any ability for you to do some of the advanced list segmentation that we've been talking about. A lot of folks have gone and paid more money and dealt with a lot more complicated admin panels with companies like Infusionsoft. I own a license to Infusionsoft. They're good people, but for a lot of folks it's just more than they really need. They want to stick with Aweber. What some of these other competitors of Aweber have done is they've made it easy for someone to send out an email to their list, and then when somebody clicks on a link in the email, they're automatically tagged and can be added to a new follow-up series. For example, let's say that you have a fitness product and most of it has had to do with how to get six-pack abs, but now you want to talk about, "I've got this product on how to shed a whole bunch of weight and how to get completely ripped." You could send out an email saying, "Look, I've got this video that you really need to see that's very controversial on the whole topic of losing weight, and why everything that you've heard about losing weight is completely wrong. Just click this link and check out the video." Of course, anyone who's interested in that topic is going to click that link. Not everyone is going to click it, but only the folks who are interested in that topic. So they click the link, and from their point of view they click the link and they arrive at a page where you have your video. There's no opt-in page barrier that you used to see. It's always been confusing to me why, if I'm on your list, you have me click a link and then opt in again. I'm already on your list.

So just imagine that someone clicked the link and they land on the page. They see the video right away. There's no friction, no barrier, and they just watch the video. Maybe you tell them to do something after that, but what's important is that behind the scenes AW Pro Tools has spoken to your Aweber account and said, "This person is interested in this topic, so let's add the custom tag of 'fat loss' to their customer record, and let's go ahead and add them to this other list where we have 20 other autoresponders set up." Seamlessly in the background they were added to another list. Aweber does not send out an email asking them if they want to be on that list. It just copies them right over, and then they start to receive those follow-up messages. This really brings together many of the things that you and I have been talking about – the list segmentation, tracking someone's behavior, and having these very focused follow-up conversations with someone based on what they do, their behavior. In a nutshell, that's what AW Pro Tools does. It does a few other things that we could talk about, but that's the core functionality, giving you the ability to segment your list even after you've already built your list, and to give you the ability to copy or add people to new follow-up sequences automatically without them knowing anything other than they clicked a link and they arrived at a page to watch your content.

BEN SETTLE: Let's talk about the other functions. I remember one of them I was looking at is it does automatic backups, which someone might not think is a big deal, but in today's day and age, all the autoresponder companies are trying to rightfully crack down on spammers and stuff and sometimes good people get caught in the crosshairs. It could happen to any autoresponder, not just Aweber.

JACK BORN: Absolutely. I've got it set up in AW Pro Tools where you have the option to have the system automatically do an off-site backup of your entire list. What happens is that every night it grabs all the new folks that were added to your list. The first time you do it, it does a massive backup of your entire list, even if it's 100,000 records. It will back up the whole thing off-site and it encrypts all the data using the same level of encryption that the NSA uses. If you're not familiar with the NSA, that's the United States spy agency that makes the CIA and FBI look like kids. These are the guys that are eavesdropping on phone calls and things like that. It uses the same encryption to make sure that it's all safe and secure. However, if you need that backup for whatever reason whatsoever, it's available for you. I like to think of it as insurance. It's nice to have that back-up just in case, because you've heard many times that the value of your business is really in the list. Having that resource available to you if something were to go wrong is a nice insurance. One of the other tools that are in there is the ability to set up what I call an automation robot, so let me explain that. An automation robot is very similar to what I described about the segmentation when someone clicks a link, except instead of someone clicking a link, this is triggered when someone arrives at the end of your autoresponder series. Again it's completely optional. You can use it or not use it, but if you set it up, what happens is when someone reaches the end of say a 20-series autoresponder sequence, the very next day you can either tag their account or copy them to a new list or just move them to a new list.

BEN SETTLE: That's so cool. That solves so many problems.

JACK BORN: It helps you keep your list clean. This is one of those types of tools where I knew that folks were going to be able to use it in lots of creative different ways, so there's really dozens of different ways that somebody could use this. I just received a request in my help desk today where someone was using, like you do, the radio talk show model. But then they want to be able to send them an email with a link in it using AW Pro Tools to be able to send them to a completely different follow-up series. Wouldn't it be great if they could click that link and all the sudden they're having this conversation? Maybe it's five or six emails where they're having this conversation. They're paused on the other list, so they're not receiving additional communication, but now based on their behavior they're having this focused conversation to see if they want to buy this product after you've had this focused conversation. Whether they do or whether they don't, you re-start the other autoresponder series. That's where AW Pro Tools is going to. It's not quite there yet, but that's the direction that I'm headed, to give you the ability to basically let your subscribers choose their own adventure. You don't have to tell them that, but based on their behavior, what they receive day by day will change. Your follow-up marketing will automatically shift and change, based on your subscriber's behavior. It's very powerful because it's like this artificial intelligence machine that, once you set it up, is going to modify the follow-up messages based on what people do.

BEN SETTLE: That "choose your own adventure" thing, I first heard that terminology in January or February 2012. We tried to implement this with a weight loss info publishing company I was a partner in at the time, and we could never quite make it work because with Aweber you'd have to manually go in and move people every 30 days or however long. It was really manual. If you can pull that off, I think that is the ideal way to do it.

JACK BORN: Just to be clear, the part where someone clicks a link and they're added to a new autoresponder list or they're copied to a new autoresponder list, that already works. We've been doing that for clients for over four months, so that already exists. The part that I was referring to is where basically when someone is moved to a new list, they're automatically paused on the existing list, but you can get them restarted on the main list automatically. That's what I'm getting to. I'll run through some of the other tools and also some of the things that are just over the horizon. Also, inside of AW Pro Tools there's a stats panel so you can see unique clicks and raw clicks. Also, there's some tools that really don't specifically have to do with Aweber, but I still think they're very powerful. One of them is the ability to copy and paste your email into this text area, and it will format that email in such a way that it looks great whether someone's reading it on a big computer screen or they're reading it on their mobile phone. I'm seeing emails come out all the time, I'm sure you are too, where I'm reading them on my iPhone and it has this really funky ugly distracting layout. It's a complete sentence from left to right, then the next line is two words, then all the way across, then a word. That's a symptom of doing these hard breaks, whether it's Aweber, or I see this a lot with Infusionsoft actually, where you say, "The hard break is at this point, after this many characters." When someone's reading that on their iPhone it just looks kind of odd and mangled. It really screams, "This is a marketing email. Ben didn't sit down and write out an email and send it to me." My tool makes it so that it looks great whether it's on your computer or whether it's on a smart phone.

A few other things that are in there is the ability to use some algorithms to apply a grade to the email, not in terms of how good the copywriting is, but in terms of what grade level of intelligence is written to. The idea there is that you want to target somewhere around the 5th to 7th or 8th grade level. You want to keep it in that range. If you type in or paste in your email and it's at the 12th grade level or higher, that's a sign that you're probably going to lose some people because you're speaking over their head. Another one is the ability to add funky symbols to subject lines, which I would recommend that you use sparingly. It's things like a heart shape or a thumbs-up. You can add those to subject lines. The final one that I put in there recently is you can go to YouTube and grab anyone's YouTube video link, whether it's yours or someone else's, and copy and paste it into the text field. It will create the HTML for you to put a thumbnail of that YouTube video right in your email, so here's how you would use it. If you had a YouTube video on a blog post or a page, even if it's someone else's video, as long as it's on the page that they arrive at after they click your link, a good way to increase the clickthroughs is for you to send out an email that for the most part looks like text, but then there's one image. It says, "Click the video below to watch this video." With an email like that, they're going to see the actual thumbnail of the video. It's going to look clickable, so they can click on it. What it does, rather than playing in the email, it sends them back to your page where the video will be, where they can watch it.

BEN SETTLE: Are there any other features?

JACK BORN: I can talk about what's coming. One of the things that's coming is the ability to set up some code on a thank-you page, so when somebody makes a purchase they're automatically added to a buyer's list. This is a feature where, regardless of the platform – whether it's PayPal, 1ShoppingCart, your own merchant account, or whatever it is – as soon as they hit that thank-you page they would automatically be added to the buyer's list. You would have this list of people who've bought from you one or more times, so you'd be able to go inside Aweber and pull up your list of buyers and mail to them. That's a very, very powerful feature that people are going to really enjoy. There's another one that I'm working on. I haven't quite figured out some of the details about exactly how this will work, but I know that it's technically possible. The idea is that when someone clicks the link in the email, you could have them automatically registered to GoToWebinar. They're added to your list, they're tagged, and they're subscribed to GoToWebinar, all in one click. This has been fascinating, Jack, it really has. And if someone reading this wants a free test drive of Jack Born's AW Pro Tools, and a 20% discount if you decide to buy it, use my affiliate link below:

www.EmailPlayers.com/awprotools

Chapter 5
How to Generate
All the Traffic and Leads
Your Greedy Little Heart Desires
Using Solo Ads

BEN SETTLE: Tell us who you are and what you do.

IGOR KHEIFETS: I'm a full-time marketer. I've been working from home close to four years now, but overall trying to make money online for way over that. In fact, I spent the first 3 or 3-1/2 years not really making anything, not making money at all, nothing worth writing home about. I definitely couldn't quit my day job.

To describe myself, I'm the Solo Guy. I guess people know me as Igor the Solo Guy. Of course, if you guys don't know what a solo is, it's sort of this niche type of traffic source that's still really unfamiliar to a lot of people out there. It's a sophisticated version of an email drop, where you pay a list owner, someone that has a mailing list. Actually, that means that anyone who has a mailing list can sell solo, which is the coolest part, and you can turn it into an income stream.

Solo is when you pay a list owner to mail his list, usually the list that he commits to delivering a specific number of visitors from his list to your offer. The more sophisticated people will also commit to a time frame. I know a lot of people who will commit to delivering you 1,000 visitors in less than a day and that's the deal. If they fail you can actually claim your money back, which kind of takes the risk away almost from your traffic purchases.

BEN SETTLE: How did you get into doing solo ads specifically? Had you played around with some other traffic stuff and this is just the thing that worked? Or you just liked writing solo ads? Why solo ads for you?

IGOR KHEIFETS: In a nutshell it's all about predictability, both in terms of getting the traffic you paid for and knowing exactly what to expect. I've been using solo ads for well over three years now, and month-in and month-out I know exactly what to expect from my traffic purchases.

On the contrary, Facebook ads, which is something I do as well, my lead cost can be as little as $1.50 or $1.15 for a really amazing ad campaign, all the way up to $50 a lead. It ranges and it varies a whole lot and really depends on a lot of stuff. With solo ads, I'm acting in a very predictable space.

As far as why solo ads and in terms of how did I end up in solo ads, I actually kind of stumbled upon solo ads, to be honest, because when I was just getting that momentum up and I started making a little money, there were no solo ads per se. There was no traffic source known as solo ads. You couldn't just go out there and Google "email solo ads" and find people.

There were perhaps maybe two or three people like myself who sold solo ads, and you couldn't really find them, like I said. You needed to be a member of some sort of Skype chat room, like a private mastermind room where people would talk about this, but again it wasn't something that people would talk about mainstream.

I started working with this fellow by the name of Jayson Benoit, who is a guy who created Quality Click Control, which is a tracking and cloaking software, really useful stuff if you are getting into solo ads. He kind of told me, "You can sell a solo ad." I'm like, "What does that mean? How do I sell one? How do I buy one?"

He introduced me to these people, and eventually I was one of the folks who took solo ads mainstream by educating other marketers that there is this traffic source where you get predictable clicks at an affordable rate, that doesn't have any limitations like Facebook and PPC have. If you do Google advertising you can no longer take a visitor from the ad to a squeeze page. You have to do a fake blog and put content on it, so there's little distractions going on. If you do get like a 15% optin rate from your promotion where you pay $3 or $5 per click, you're supposed to be very, very happy. On Facebook on the other hand it's almost the same thing. You can link to a squeeze page, sure, but you can't really make any claims. If you're in the biz opp or make money online space or you want to promote an affiliate link to a Clickbank product, which is something a lot of people like to do, you're very limited. You cannot do that.

Some people will even go ahead and cloak their links, and the people who approve the ad will see some sort of legitimate website that makes no claim whatsoever. Then when they approve it, they switch it over to the illegal site, so eventually they get their account shut down.

With solo ads in that regard, there are no limitations besides the limitation that the list owner will put on you, and usually those are very moderate. They allow you to make claims. They don't put you in a cage or in this box where you can't really say the word 'money' or you can't make any promises or propositions that are sexy, the sort of propositions that people are responsive to. Anything that even remotely looks like a business opportunity or make money online products, or information products in the internet marketing space, usually get shut down.
In fact, they can do it with other markets as well. If you follow guys like Don Wilson, the Facebook ads guy, he's been reporting that they've just switched the rules on the Teespring so you can't really promote Teespring now, or there's some sort of twist to it at this point. Last month everyone was making a killing with Teespring, so the more people that get onto this thing, the more limiting the circumstances become for advertisers.

Now, like I said with solo ads that's not the case. The only issue you're facing is that the guy or the gal that you're buying traffic from can probably get booked up ahead for a while, so you have to wait until they can mail out.

BEN SETTLE: Most of the people listening or reading this transcript will understand what a solo ad is, but just in case someone doesn't, how would you define a solo ad, just so everybody knows exactly what you mean by that.

IGOR KHEIFETS: A solo ad is a single email to someone's list that is within the same area of interest as your offer is. If you're promoting an offer about making money as an affiliate marketer, you can get a solo ad where a guy who owns a list that is interested in that will email the list, and you will pay only per click delivered. You will pay up front and you decide if you want to get 100 clicks or 200 or 300 or 500, that's up to you. Most solo ad sellers will offer packages ranging between 50 and 1,000 probably. You pay them up front, and let's just say you've agreed to pay 50 cents a click for 100 clicks, so you pay the guy literally $50 and he delivers the clicks by mailing to his list. If he fails to deliver on the first send, he'll probably have to re-email the list again the next day to deliver. Of course, given the fact that it's very easy to lose reputation, he has to deliver or he's risking losing customers. The solo industry is very open. Everyone knows everyone and if you mess with one client, soon enough you lose your reputation, which is something that very few sellers want to do.

BEN SETTLE: You've been doing this for a while now and you're pretty well known for this. What are some mistakes people make with their solo ads that you've seen?

IGOR KHEIFETS: Do you mean buying them?

BEN SETTLE: That's one question, but just generally what mistakes are people making? For example, before the call you and I briefly talked and I said, "Hey, I might be interested in your solo ads," and you explained to me, "You need something more generalized." Like it would have been a mistake for me to run an ad.

IGOR KHEIFETS: I understand where you're coming from. The biggest mistake – or it might not be the biggest, but it might be the most expensive mistake that anyone can make is not understanding the market before hitting solo ads.

Let's just take an example. I guess the people listening to this call are mostly internet marketers, so I'm assuming we're all familiar with a place called the Warrior Forum. The Warrior Forum is a place where you've got semi-advanced people, so if you post about squeeze pages or say something like, "Here's a squeeze page building software," most people will know what you're talking about, but when we're talking about solo ads we need to assume that they know absolutely nothing. All they've got is this desire to make money from home. That's really who the prospect is. This is where they are right now.

To give you an example from a different industry, if you listen to Zig Ziglar and you go to his seminar, he's still telling you those pots and pans stories and going door to door and selling cookies like the Girl Scouts etc, because this is where his audience is. This is the level where his audience is located at. Therefore, he has to cater to that.

When we're talking solo ads, selling something sophisticated like a backlink software or a squeeze page software or even something that's targeted towards people doing SEO optimization is really not it, because these guys aren't at that level yet. Many of them are not good at technical stuff. They have perhaps no clue what copywriting means. A lot of them don't have an understanding of what a sales funnel is.

When I buy solo ads, I'm explaining these concepts on my sales page because without me explaining them the reader might not even understand the value behind the product sometimes. But because I operate in that list building sub-niche of the big make money online market, I now have to pull these prospects – who are interested in list building and who understand that the money's in the list – in through my copy.

I've actually spent a lot of time on this and it's cost me tens of thousands of dollars to figure this out until it really hit me like a speeding train that they are general. Like I said, it's a very general market and what they want is that shortcut to make money from home. That's pretty much the ultimate product, the silver bullet, which is incidentally not that different from a big segment of our market anywhere.

I guess with solo ads what's important to mention is that they will not understand sophisticated terms, so you have to explain to them what they are. Expecting them to know this or assuming that they understand a lot of these terms is going to be a big mistake that's going to cost you the sale, and that you don't want to make.

BEN SETTLE: That sounds like really good advice. I've used solo ads in other markets, but they've always been generalized markets like weight loss and that sort of thing. I've never tried it in mine, and I'm kind of glad I'm talking to you about this. You probably just saved me a bunch of money. What about when people are buying solo ads? I've heard people explain it's kind of a swamp out there, media buying. What are some mistakes people make when they're trying to buy their solo ads?

IGOR KHEIFETS: Oh man, there's so many. Let's just go over a few fundamental ones. The first thing people do is that some people will try to send the traffic directly to an affiliate link of some product without really putting people through a squeeze page first.

As we know, most people will not buy on the first encounter of an offer. Maybe it's because they want to Google your name. Maybe they're at work right now and they can't devote the time to go through the offer. Whatever the case may be, you've got to put them on your list first and then take them to the sales presentation. Not doing that will cost you a lot of money.

Another costly mistake, and it will sound fundamental but I can't stress how common this is, is that people don't make sure that their systems are working and their tracking is in place. In other words, they might give you the link to mail to, but the tracking link is either expired or it takes them to a totally different link, which happens. At that point again you've lost a bunch of money.

Another mistake would be not working with people who are proven to be trustworthy. Ever since about a year ago there's a lot of people that are riding this solo craze. Again, I was one of the people who was responsible for taking solo mainstream, kind of educating the marketplace about solo ads even existing as a traffic source. Until then, everyone was just going to Facebook and Google and doing SEO.

What happened was a lot of people just abuse it. They create these Facebook profiles and call themselves Roy Bennett Solo Ads or Bob Jones Solo Ads, and literally creating profiles for solo ads, creating fake solo pages and literally scamming people. That's a big, big mistake, but it probably comes from not knowing and trying to save money, because the scammers will try to lure you in with a very, very cheap price.

If we're talking an average price being about 50 cents a click or so – maybe a bit higher than that, depending on who you buy from, because each and every solo ad provider can set his own pricing – the scammers will try to sell you traffic at 25 or 20 or 30 cents a click. That should raise a red flag because, first off, if they don't value their list at all and they're willing to settle for 20-25 cents a click, that means their list is crap, and that's at the very least.

At the most, it means they're just going to take your money and run, and there's been numerous accounts of this happening. I've been taken for a ride myself quite a few times. In fact, just two months ago I had about $700 tied up in this piece with sellers who did not deliver and stopped responding.

I would sincerely recommend that even though the advice sounds extremely fundamental, it's a vicious world out there, it's brutal, so you definitely want to work with people who have tons of testimonials, and not just testimonials on their website, but more so reviews of other marketers that are posting on blogs or reviews in directories.

You can go on Google and type in 'solo ad directory' and you'll find a bunch of trusted directories with a bunch of reviews out there. There's a guy, Mike from Maine, and he's been reviewing solo ads lately. There's Reed Floren's solo directory. There's a guy name Prashant, and he has Solo Ad X directory, so check these. Make sure whoever you want to buy from is listed there. Do not ever buy from someone you cannot find any reviews about.

I guess in my book even a bad review is better than no reviews at all, because if they have no reviews at all it means that they just started yesterday and they might be one of those fly-by-night or butterfly solo sales I call them, because they disappear overnight. You send them the money and then they just disappear. They start a new Paypal account, new Facebook account, new solo ad page, etc. and they just reappear again under a different name. It happens all the time.

BEN SETTLE: Here's a question I have for you. The only solo ads I've ever bought – and I don't know if this just the biz opp industry or not – but I always bought them like a flat fee. It wasn't per click you were buying for, but it was a flat fee. Do you recommend solo ads where you're paying per click as opposed to just a flat fee?

IGOR KHEIFETS: What you're referring to is actually called an email drop. That's the old-fashioned way to do solo ads. In fact, I think solos evolved from that. There used to be a time where you'd go and buy a list, like a rental list. You'd pay someone a flat fee. I think the ArcaMax people still do that.

BEN SETTLE: I just used them actually to promote my zombie novel.

IGOR KHEIFETS: Yeah, they charge you a flat fee and you give them the swipe and they mail the swipe, and whatever clicks you get, that's what you pay for. In my last promotion, I paid them I think $700 and I only got about 350 clicks, so I actually paid $2 per click, four times the average cost per click I could get on a different solo ad.

Whether or not you should go for one or the other, I don't know. That really depends on your offer and your swipe. Maybe your swipe is so amazing that you're going to pull several thousand clicks from their list. Again, going back to the predictability of the thing, that's one thing they're just missing from what we do. Whether we're talking being an entrepreneur or whether we're talking running an online business, there's a lot of unpredictable stuff.

With solo ads where you pay per click, there's predictability. I personally just love to know that if I pay someone $250 I'm getting 500 clicks, and that's at the very minimum, by the way, because most legit sellers will always over-deliver. We have this commitment with our clients that we will always over-deliver at least 10% of what they paid for, so if you order say 500 clicks with us, you always get 550 minimum to just give you better value for your money. Usually if the seller is legit you will find that happening all the time.

I personally stick to the direction of predictable cost per click because that also allows me to calculate my budget. I just know that I can allocate $10,000 this month towards solo ads, and I can expect an approximate ROI of XYZ. Therefore, at the end of the month I can do my calculations for the next month.

Predictability in this business is something I learned to value about a year and a half ago when my daughter was born. I was never a risk taker, even though today I'm more of a risk taker than I used to be, but I was always reluctant to take risks. I was very uneasy about risking my money.

With solo ads, it takes a certain level of that away, which to this day I really appreciate. Not to mention that anyone who's new to the business, it's valuable 10X because when you're starting out with a very limited budget and you need to know what exactly you should be doing with that, every penny counts.

BEN SETTLE: What are some mistakes people make if they're writing their own solo ads? I'm sure you see this a lot, actually. What are some things that make you cringe when you see people's solo ads?

IGOR KHEIFETS: I'd say they try to write these long email swipes that are nothing but hype. They're just trying to stick as many features and benefits into that email and make it ridiculously long, even though a solo seller may have sent out a similar one the day before.

I'd say that in solo ads what you want to focus on is getting as many clicks from the email swipe as possible, not so much focusing on pre-qualifying the lead, but more so treating this as this general traffic source where your job is to get the most clicks humanly possible.

Ryan Deiss talks about it a lot, and they do a lot of solo ads, too. When doing solo ads, the email is a tool to generate clicks, nothing more, nothing less. Therefore, you'll find many solo sellers operating on curiosity to get as many clicks as possible. Therefore, your squeeze page and your offer need to be doing the job of pre-qualifying them and selling them.

When doing solo ads I wouldn't say that you have this luxury of driving extremely super-duper qualified traffic. Just to compare it to say Facebook, you have your ad creative that you're running. Let's just say that your ad is displaying on the right side. You can literally target the people you want and use specific verbiage to pull that, and you only pay per click or per impression if you're doing impression marketing.

With solo ads, when the advertiser commits to delivering the amount of clicks you ordered, and more – like I said, usually they do even more – they need every click. They absolutely need every click to be pulled, and therefore they'll go towards a more generic approach. So, I recommend your squeeze page to kind of cover for that with hard-core pre-qualifying before they hit your paid offer.

BEN SETTLE: I'm thinking of Google AdWords where it's almost the opposite. You want a qualified click, but with solo ads you don't really want a qualified click. You want your page to do all the qualifying. I'm guessing you can get away with that because with a solo ad it's not like people who are not interested in that are going there. They at least have some interest. With pay per click you have click fraud and all that stuff going on.

IGOR KHEIFETS: Yeah, with pay per click you're paying a lot of money for a click, therefore you need to target buying keywords. If you're selling guitars, you can't just target keywords like *the best guitar.* You've got to target *guitar pricing.* That's a buyer keyword.

With solo ads, you just get a general crowd. You get like a herd of people going to that link, and therefore what you want to do is to get as many of them as possible. Usually these folks are geared towards opting in and responding to offers, because for a lot of them that's what they do. They just check their email all day long and click on things. That's just their reality. You definitely want to get as many of them as humanly possible on your list, then go ahead and try to sell your product.

Those who don't buy your product after say 7 to 14 days, you can start thinking of new ways to monetize them. Maybe you want to do some ad swapping to get some free traffic going on, or maybe you want to promote some affiliate offers. Maybe you want to see if a different sub-niche product will get their attention. If you're selling a copywriting-related product or an affiliate-related product, maybe you can try to sell a CPA-related product. Maybe you can try to just push a CPA offer and just get paid per action, per optin, per click, whatever.

There's many different ways to monetize those who don't buy, but you definitely want to have as many of them on your list as possible because many of them will buy after they go through your follow-up sequence. I've found that between 40-60% of my sales off solo traffic come from my follow-up sequence. That's a critical element right there.

BEN SETTLE: I've seen the same thing. I would send traffic to an offer and might get 1-2% of sales, but then when they're in the autoresponder it's like 11-12% of them convert to sales. It's a huge difference, just night and day. I'm going to change it up a little bit here. Just today I was reading something you wrote on Facebook which was pretty cool, about this guru you knew who was like on the verge of bankruptcy and you had to give him some kind of harsh advice, but I thought it was good advice that all of us can never hear too often. Can you talk about that a little bit?

IGOR KHEIFETS: For sure. This guru's a good friend of mine. I've met him a couple times in person. When I say guru, I mean because of the amount of money he used to make and as he's positioned in the industry. He's a very nice dude.

He's like hitting me on Facebook and he's like "Dude, I've got to talk to you." I'm like, "What happened?" "I've just got to talk to you, man. Just give me your cell phone."

I'm not really big on giving my cell phone to people because I try to keep things as [inaudible] as possible, just working out of my little coffee shop. I don't own the coffee shop but I work out of one because my wife won't let me work from home. She's always bucking this stuff.

So, I'm giving him my cell phone number, he calls me up, and he told me something that really shocked me. My jaw was on the floor for a few minutes until I kind of shook it off and helped him. He said that he had about $200 left to his name, and that's not really enough to last him till the end of the week and that he just doesn't know what to do.

He went on to even offer me equity in the business in exchange for me helping him bring the business up, which I didn't take because I didn't feel like taking advantage of that situation, but I did give him some harsh advice. All the credit goes to him for implementing, by the way, which is an important point. You've actually got to do stuff to make things happen, so he did it the same that I told him and he pocketed $15,000 in the next 48 hours.

What he was focusing on was he was running these ads and he couldn't make the money back, so he would try to get me to share on, "How the hell do I go about minimizing the cost per lead?" and that's one of the biggest things that I've noticed in the marketplace in the recent month. Everyone wants free leads. Everyone wants low-cost leads. Anyone who's into Facebook marketing, they always talk about 2-cent Likes and 1-cent this and 5-cent that.

I find this to be ridiculous because how can you make money with a 5-cent Like? I mean how do you make money with a Like? That just doesn't make any sense. In the game of direct response, which is essentially what we're doing here because we're literally buying the leads – the lead is never free, the lead always costs us something – while most people focus on trying to minimize that cost and spend as little money as they can on advertising and not risk their budget, what I'm encouraging my students to do is to figure out a way to spend as much money as they possibly can on the lead.

If you can spend $1 on a lead and I can spend $5, I'll make you look stupid. They won't even want to do business with you because of how amazing I'll look in their eyes. Usually those who figure that one out – "How do I spend more per lead, but at the same time get 5-15X more per lead than I spent?" – those are the ones who advance forward, and that's exactly what this guru dude did. He just took my advice.

I told him to completely change the proposition and shift the focus of what he was offering. I actually did ask him to pitch me on the phone. What he was offering I thought was, for lack of a better word, extremely weak. It's not a proposition that I'd respond to if I had the money, so he changed the proposition. He actually didn't spend any money on that one, by the way. I've got to confess here. He had a list of about 400-500 people that purchased his products in the past, and we're talking about a list that was up to six months old.

I asked him, "Did you market to that list? Did you send that proposition to that list?" and he said, "Well yeah, but nobody responded." Once we changed the proposition – and I'm talking about literally twisting it upside down from what he had – he had 20 responses. Out of those 20 responses I think he signed up either 8 or 12 clients, so each of them paid him several thousand dollars. Within 48 hours I got a message from him on Facebook that he just killed it. He went on vacation shortly after that, spending that money.

This transformation that can happen to your business when you make the shift in your focus can literally be instantaneous. Things can change in a heartbeat if you just do your marketing right and get your head together.

BEN SETTLE: What I like about that story is it's not that you taught him some secret ninja thing. You just went back to the fundamentals of direct response marketing. It can move mountains, just doing the fundamentals over and over. People lose sight of that and it was a good lesson. It was interesting.

IGOR KHEIFETS: If you look at marketing – Ben, I'm sure you'll agree with me here – look at marketing ever since the ebook was invented. Every single piece of salesmanship we see, every single piece of marketing we see hasn't changed one bit. Even though as marketers we always try to sell this innovative solution, usually it's a very simplistic solution to a complicated problem, at least that's what gets you the most money, selling simplistic solutions to complicated problems. The wheel hasn't been reinvented.

The way I see this to pan out is the books that are the oldest about direct response copywriting, the books that were written 50-60 years ago or 30 years ago like *Scientific Advertising* – I don't know when that was written, but many principles of *Scientific Advertising* I see being applied everywhere online.

My entire business is based on the classics of direct response, studying guys like John Carlton, Dan Kennedy, Gary Bencivenga, and anyone else. Let's take one of the biggest gurus online in our marketplace right now, Frank Kern. Maybe Rich Schefren is bigger than he is, but when it comes to IM, Frank Kern is the god, the guru, the prophet.

Frank Kern learned most of his stuff from Dan Kennedy, and if you really dissect his marketing it's all direct response. It's salesmanship in print, or sometimes it's on video, just basically reading a script on video that was printed at one point. His propositions are fairly irresistible through positioning he's created.

Again, the market hasn't changed. The wheel has not been reinvented in the last couple of decades. It's just, like you said, Ben, we tend to lose track of that and we keep on looking for the greatest shiny object.

I have to admit, though, solo ads as a traffic source has only been developed about three years ago or so, and we took it mainstream about a year or year and a half ago, maybe a bit more than that, but the essentials to making money are still the same. It's traffic that's going to an irresistible offer that creates conversions which equals money. That's the formula. There's no secret formula to making money online. That is the recipe.

If you're not making any, one of them is screwed up. Either your traffic sucks or your proposition sucks. Most of the time, by the way, it's the proposition, because you can make money even with crappy traffic if your proposition is irresistible.

BEN SETTLE: Now I want to talk more about your solo ad services. Tell us about that. I just saw your stuff, dude, just a couple weeks ago when we first met. I read about it and I've been sending some of my friends there. I don't know if they've been buying from you or not, but I think there's a lot of people who are going to be reading this transcript that might be able to use what you've got, so tell us a little bit about your solo ad service.

IGOR KHEIFETS: Okay. First, I appreciate the referrals you've been sending me. I really, really appreciate that. In fact, most of my business is referrals. That's how my business really grows, and I hope I can serve your guys right.

To tell you about my service, what we do is we help you get traffic. We examine your offer and if it's any good we'll help you get traffic to it. We'll even help you craft your proposition. We're not going to write your sales page for you, but we'll definitely consult with you on whether or not there's a fit. We'll recommend the right traffic source and we even offer buyer solos at this point, which is something nobody else out there does. You can mail to my buyer list, people who've bought my info products and bought my coaching program.

If you really insist I can even mail your solo to the people who bought my solo ads, which is a very responsive list, but your proposition has to be irresistible. It has to be really, really useful to my people, so that's a whole different conversation because I do take real careful care of those customers. They're pretty much my most valuable gold customers, and I don't really give access to them just to anyone.

In a nutshell, that's what we do. We help you identify whether or not your proposition is any good for a solo ad, and if it is we help you with traffic. If it isn't, we just either send you to a place where you might find success, or we instruct you on how to tweak your proposition to get the best ROI with solo ad traffic.

BEN SETTLE: You mentioned you have a buyers list, too. Between those lists that you have, what kinds of businesses are a good fit for your service, just so people don't waste your time if they're in the wrong niche or whatever. Who's good for your service?

IGOR KHEIFETS: That's a very good question, but it's also a very complicated one to answer, so let me try to answer it in a bit of a different way. Let me tell you the offers that are not a good fit. Usually SEO-related offers, where you sell SEO services, and design services, like if you're a web designer and you want to get clients to work with you, that is not a good fit.

What fits best is if you – I don't want to say you sell magic potions and magic buttons, because nobody wants that; that's just not something that actually exists – but if you're selling a legitimate strategy on making money from home, if you have traffic-related products, if you have affiliate marketing-related products, or if you're just an affiliate for a business opportunity of some sort, or maybe you're promoting a product launch – like some people make their living off of promoting other people's launches and they hit leader boards and stuff like that – if you're doing that we can help you, too, especially with our buyer list.

In fact, one of my clients landed on a leader board alongside Daegan Smith, Andrew Fox, and a couple other big marketers like Russell Brunson, just by having me mail his offer to our buyer list, which generated like 19 sales for him. That was a very good match. He was promoting a program called YouTube Tsunami, which is a business opportunity by Paul Lynch. He had this big launch and rallied people up, so definitely if you're an affiliate it's a great fit.

If you're a business opportunity marketer, if you have any sort of sales funnel building software perhaps, maybe you promote these products like Lead System Pro, so you sign up and you're able to make squeeze pages and stuff like that, that was a great fit, too.

Incidentally, MLM'ers have a lot of success with our traffic, but of course the MLM has to be legit and we'll examine that. We will not just mail it. We basically may choose not to run your offer, so in that case you might want to reach out to us by email or by contact form on our website to ask us whether or not we accept it. By the way, even if you've never done solos before, you can still reach out because we can help you get into that. Don't let that stop you.

Many of our clients, in fact about 60% of our clients, are newbies who had never run solo ads ever in their life. They're just getting into it, they're discovering it, so we'd be happy to assist you there and take you by the hand and help you not make a lot of costly mistakes, and save you a bunch of money, a bunch of time, and a bunch of frustration. I've seen it before. I've seen people losing thousands of dollars and learning costly marketing lessons without really allowing anyone to hand-hold them on their very first one.

BEN SETTLE: What link can somebody go to to read more about it? I've seen your site. You've got a ton of testimonials on there, so that's really cool. Where can they find out more about you?

IGOR KHEIFETS: They can either Google my name – Igor Kheifets – and add the words *solo ads* and they will find a bunch of reviews and a bunch of links pointing to my website probably. Or they can simply go to www.igorsoloads.com, just Igor and the words soloads.com, no dashes, just one word, and they'll be redirected to my website.

There you can not only check out all these massive testimonials, including quite a few industry leaders as well, but also, you'll be able to learn more about what solo ads are and how they work. Also, I recommend you check our solo insurance, which is where we will actually commit to helping you generate a certain optin rate – not just clicks but optin rate on your offer, or you don't pay.

We noticed a lot of people actually don't do solo ads because they're afraid of not knowing what they're doing, so what we do now for anyone who's buying for the first time, in their very first traffic campaign we work with them to help them create their very first squeeze page, and we commit to a minimum of 25% optin rate, so there's literally zero risk when you get started with solo ads for the first time. Again, we're only doing this because we noticed that over 60% of our clients are newbies. When I saw newbies, they're solo newbies. They might be experienced marketers who've never done that before. You'd be amazed how many marketers actually go for years and make tons of money, but never ever attempting something like list-building, which was again a big shocker to me and my team.

Like I said, what we do is we take the risk away and we help you get started with basically a sure-fire campaign to help you get optins and help you get people on your list so you can start marketing to them.

BEN SETTLE: Sounds good, man. Igor, I appreciate this. This has been great. Thank you.

IGOR KHEIFETS: My pleasure. Thank you.

Chapter 6
How to Get the News Media to Do All the "Heavy Lifting" of Building Your Email List for You

BEN SETTLE: This is Ben Settle of www.BenSettle.com and today I'm talking to Mike Dolpies. Mike is one of my favorite under-the-radar business experts who's also a public speaker, author, and a radio show host. He's also in one of the mastermind groups I'm in, and I've had a lot of chances to talk to him about business and publicity and that sort of thing. He is no fluke when it comes to business, by the way. He's not like the rest of us kitchen table people. Mike actually generated his first seven figures before he was 24 years old in a real brick and mortar business, and he's not an overnight so-called internet success story. He's gotten praise from guys like Ben Gay III from *The Closer* series, and Brian Tracy. His big way of making money these days is PR. He's gotten on prestigious media outlets like Fox and Entrepreneur magazine and a whole bunch of other ones, but these days apparently, he's focusing on local media, as that's where the real money is, so that's what we're going to talk about.

Mike, thank you for showing up today.

MIKE DOLPIES: Hey, Ben. It's good to be talking with your listeners and your readers, and hopefully we can help them out.

BEN SETTLE: We'll start out with a question I've wanted to ask you actually. I love PR. I love the whole idea, but I haven't done a whole lot of it. I've done enough of it to see how cool it can be. Why local media as opposed to the big national ones? Why is that better for most of us?

MIKE DOLPIES: There's a few things. One is it kind of comes back down to the big fish in a little pond theory. It's obviously easier to stand out in your local market than it is to penetrate and stand out in the bigger market – although of course if you're on bigger outlets, like let's say the national Fox News channel or Good Morning America or any big network, it gives you enormous credibility.

You're not going to take one over the other, but here's the deal. The local media has to be done and mastered. I've been a martial arts guy for a lifetime, and what's that all about? It's all about moving up the ranks. I just sent somebody an email today, a good mentor of ours, Paul Hartunian. Unless you have a pet rock or the Brooklyn Bridge, you're not going to get to the national outlets as fast as you want to do it, so you have to lay the groundwork locally.

You master that locally and you practice locally and it becomes so easy in a way. Then you look like, "Hey, this guy's a pro or this girl's a pro." That's what you can do with local media. Then when it's time for you to step up to the national stage, guess what. You're just going to be so ready. You're not going to be like *8 Mile* and Eminem – you've got one shot, one opportunity. You're going to be able to blow it up when you get that shot and get that opportunity, and you're going to end up creating it anyway.

There's a lot of reasons why local media is powerful, but that's just one. Does that make sense?

BEN SETTLE: It does make sense. Will the information you're going to give us apply to people who are not necessarily selling locally? Maybe they're on the internet and they're selling to people in other countries for all we know. Does this all apply?

MIKE DOLPIES: It does, because these things live on. You're going to get local media whether you're selling something that can be sold across state borders, across the seven seas if you want, and it's going to help you sell those for sure.

Here's the deal. We all have to live somewhere, so in a way we're all local, because we all live somewhere. Some people choose to be hermits or choose not to go out and network, and that's fine, that's a choice, but the truth is we still have to live somewhere. What better way to network or connect with people than to be seen on TV or heard on the radio, and you really don't have to do much to do that, except for know what to do to get it.

We just all have to live somewhere, so that's why media applies to anybody, because we're all local. Would you sell an email marketing course or your newsletter to your neighbor and subscribe him? If he was a good prospect you would, so [inaudible] locally too.

BEN SETTLE: It's just as easy to sell something like that to someone who lives 2,000 miles away as it is to someone who lives 2 feet away. The order button's going to be the same. It's not more of an effort for them to click the link because they live farther away.

MIKE DOLPIES: Right, it's all the same. That's really what it comes down to. I have clients that are here locally in the state I live, and I have clients that are in different parts of the country and world. It applies everywhere.

BEN SETTLE: Now let me ask you this question, if you don't mind. How much profit has local PR brought you? You don't have to give an exact number, but just as opposed to other ways of marketing you've done. Is it a big chunk of it? Is it better than traditional advertising or is it about the same? How does that fit in your world right now?

MIKE DOLPIES: I told this to Doberman Dan. I said, "Dan, you sit down and we all sit down and we do our sales letters and we do our marketing pieces," and I do a lot of direct mail too, so I sit down and craft my direct mail pieces and I do my ads for the magazines and my emails and my website and all that kind of stuff.

What you're doing for PR is not that much different than what you do when you sit down and do your marketing anyway. What you're going to do, though, is you have to take about 60% of what you do in your marketing and you have to kind of throw away the other 40%, and then you have to add the 40%, which is kind of the PR ingredients. Then you end up with kind of getting your same message out, but in a public relations, local celebrity media-type mentality.

That's #1. Basically, you're going to do this anyway, and one way to measure your PR is you measure it in what it would cost you. If you get a five-minute segment on the local network affiliate, just do the math on how much that would actually cost if you'd actually buy five minutes of commercial time, or 30 minutes on the radio, or I have an hour radio show once a week. How much would that actually cost, or how much does it cost to get a full-page spread in a local business publication or a local parenting magazine, whatever your target market is. That's one way to measure that, and we've heard all the gurus talk about that.

The other way to measure it is actually the real dollars in the bank, and I'll just give you a few examples off the top of my head. I kind of fall under the category that we all kind of gel together in our little mastermind group that we hang around in. We all have good strengths and expertise.

There's probably not one of us that's really that great at kind of the analytical tracking standpoint. Maybe I'm just assuming, but I know I'm not the greatest. I usually rely on my memory, which is pretty darn good. I did some math, and I've seen clients who are on average worth about $13,000/year to my business, that I've been working with for the past three years, that came from an article spread that came out in a trade publication.

Then I've tracked where that particular client also referred me to another person that spends about $13,000/year, so do the math on that, and they've both been going for a while. And it's funny, but I just talked to that woman today and she introduced me to somebody else who's got something going on, and they want to maybe do something, so who knows what that door will open up.

And then there's a lot of odds and ends. There are people who have read articles in local publications that have come on board.

I'm not going to blow it up and say, "Oh, it's seven figures." I'm going to say it's easily into the six figures, and I've only been looking at PR aggressively for the last 14 months, and before that I got some exposure in my local trade publications going back a couple years.

That's when I gave you that example and that story, but it's easily over six figures, probably close to $200,000. Like I said, that's only over the course of a couple years.

Is it like a guru number or a million dollars? No, it's not. I'm giving you real numbers here that I can think of off the top of my head.

BEN SETTLE: Now how easy is it for someone who's just starting out in the business? They don't have a reputation or anything and they think, "Why would anybody want to interview me for TV or the newspaper or magazine?" Can they still do this, or do they have to have any pre-experience?

MIKE DOLPIES: Obviously if they're in business, they're in business. That's it right there. A lot of entrepreneurs don't understand this, and it took me awhile to understand this too.

The average working schmoe – even if you're working and building your business part-time – the average working corporate employee, even if they have a nice cushy executive job, they still respect people that have their own business, even if that person is just starting out in their own business and just struggling to get it going.

Everybody just has this enormous respect for people that have their own business, so your initial credo or your initial title of how do you get your foot in the door, a lot of people say, "Oh, you need a book," and books are great, they help, but you don't.

Just the fact that you're the owner of a particular business, owner of a particular company, or you do a certain thing, you're a professional at a certain thing – I mean if you're a chiropractor just starting off and you went to chiropractic school and you learned about the human body and how to whack and crack it so it feels better, that's your credibility and that's obviously what you're going to talk about in the media. Does that make sense?

BEN SETTLE: It sure does. One question people will always ask, and I remember I used to think this question too until I learned about it and actually did it and realized the truth of the matter, does somebody have to be a good speaker or presenter to do PR?

MIKE DOLPIES: It's a double-edged sword, because if you're not somewhat polished – what you need to do is you need to rehearse. I just read one of Dan Kennedy's newsletters yesterday about the sales people who never practice what to say when they come to an objection, or they never practice their script. They've got to do this stuff.

You practice every day by sending emails out. We practice our marketing and we're professionals at that and we study it. What people have to realize too is that they do have to do some practice with this.

If they're writing articles or they're being interviewed on the radio or they're being written up – obviously, there's not a lot of practice that has to go into being interviewed by a newspaper. The reporter asks you questions and you answer them and you're done pretty much, so that probably doesn't apply.

But radio, television, local TV – we could talk about details if you want. You don't have to rehearse for hours a day, but you've got to be able to get your point across. This is really off the cuff that we're having this interview today, but to get your point across well, especially in a short period of time, it's a good idea to practice it.

When I get on TV, what I do is I'll work out the segment. I'll go through the segment and I'll just pretend I'm the reporter and I'll ask myself a question and then I'll answer it. I'll set my timer app on my Android phone for how long the segment's going to be, and I'll ask the questions and I'll answer it, I'll ask a question and I'll answer it, and maybe I'll do that once a day for a week. We're talking about five minutes a day leading up a TV interview.

Is that worth it, five minutes a day to be prepared for a TV interview so you get invited back, so you come across really well on television? Absolutely. That's what you want to do. You want to prepare. You don't have to be great, but preparation beats natural talent a lot.

BEN SETTLE: It's been a few years since I've done those, but when I wrote my dog book I just started getting on the radio, and the first time was so nerve wracking. It was the stupidest thing. I don't think anybody was listening, it was such a small station.

You were talking about how much they charge and everything. I think these people only charged like $8 for advertising. [laughing] It was just a conversation. I mean you have to know your subject matter, but you already do.

MIKE DOLPIES: Yeah, it's assumed that you know your subject matter, but even when we do – like I know my subject matter now, but I'm just like anybody else, I get nervous all the time and I think nerves are healthy. I'm nervous right now talking to you – not nervous like, "Oh man, it's Ben…."

BEN SETTLE: I am an intimidating guy, it's true. [laughing]

MIKE DOLPIES: No, seriously, nerves come across in a good way, like "Hey, there's people that are going to read this, people are going to listen to this, and we want to live up to whatever hype we're going to talk about as to why people should listen to this interview."

That's where the nerves come from, and then of course that it's kind of off-the-cuff, but for the most part everybody is going to be a little nervous, if you want to use that word, doing anything.

Sometimes it's just the fact that the camera goes on. I get nervous when my wife holds a Flip camera for me at times when I do a quick little YouTube video. It's just natural.

You've seen me on television. Do I look like I'm the guy who gets nervous when my wife holds the Flip camera? I don't, but I actually do.

Again, I'm just as quirky and inadequate as the next guy. You just have to rehearse. You have to practice. It's worth it for radio, it's worth it for television. Radio's probably a little more forgiving, but again, especially for TV, you've got to rehearse a little bit. It involves taking five minutes out of your day for maybe a week.

I'm like the kid who listened to the teacher years ago, and that's probably the only thing I got from the school was, "Hey, if you want to do good on the test, start studying Tuesday for the test that's on Friday."

That's one of the best things I got from my traditional education, because I use it all the time. If you want to do good on Monday's segment, start practicing Tuesday of the previous week.

BEN SETTLE: One of the things I noticed when I was doing some PR, and I've noticed other people will say this too – and I don't know if it's the same with TV, but I'm going to assume it's even more so with TV – is the hosts don't want you to fail and flap around, so they actually assist you through the interview.

They're not trying to get you to screw up. They want you to make them look good. Is that true?

MIKE DOLPIES: I'm sure Sarah Palin would argue this....

BEN SETTLE: But I mean the average person.

MIKE DOLPIES: I know what you mean. The average guy, you're on this show, you're going to ask good questions. You're going to ask questions to kind of put me on the spot, which are going to be good for your readers. You're looking out for your readers and listeners, but you're also not going to do things that are going to jeopardize the outcome of that.

That's the same thing that's going to happen with a normal TV reporter or radio show host or whatever, a newspaper reporter – they want you to come out good because they have content they've got to put out there, and they have readers. Again, unless you're talking about the highest level with tabloids and people who have agendas in the media – which again, probably anyone who's listening to this is not at that level; I'm not at that level, I know that, to have to worry about anyone trying to corner me – but imagine Tiger Woods going on the Pope's TV. The Pope's probably going to have some tough questions for Tiger.

Every outlet is not like that. A great example again is Charlie Gibson and Sarah Palin. People who are Sarah Palin fans are looking and saying, "Man, he really cornered her.

He really tried to make her look bad. What was that all about?" And people who are Gibson fans are like, "Yeah, go get em!" For the most part, you're not going to be put under that kind of scrutiny.

BEN SETTLE: You've done a lot of TV. All I've done is radio. That's why I find this so fascinating. With radio, it was like they wouldn't even respond to your press release unless the reporter themselves was interested in that subject matter and really wanted to know more about it just for their own benefit.

MIKE DOLPIES: Right, they had to do a show that was targeted towards that subject matter. There's a few different ways to narrow your targets too, in terms of general approaches where you could definitely fit into a generalized show, and those can be very powerful, or like you were saying, the show is totally based on that topic.

We're talking about a topic that applies to entrepreneurs here, no matter what. We already cleared it out and said you don't have to be local to benefit from this. You're getting publicity, but you're starting locally first and you're going to increase your odds, and here's how to do it. This applies to copywriters, this applies to chiropractors, this applies to massage therapists and personal trainers and web designers.

BEN SETTLE: One question I have, from looking at the information you sent me, what I found really interesting – I can't wait to put you on the spot and grill you about this and make you nervous – is you don't seem to be a big fan of using press releases, right?

MIKE DOLPIES: Nope.

BEN SETTLE: Okay, so what do you do instead?

MIKE DOLPIES: Maybe I just haven't seen the light on press releases. I don't know if you want to know why I don't use press releases. What I do first is I'll throw a pitch out there, and here's the really cool thing about doing publicity.

Someone told me when I first started off, someone who kind of ran a media company but kind of didn't know how to get media because they didn't have their own track record, but I guess they were an expert or studied in college, who knows –

One thing she told me was true. I didn't notice it at first, but she said, "Media begets media." I'm thinking, "All right, I'm going to go do my first newspaper interview, and then I'm going to get calls from all the newspapers." It didn't happen that way. Here's how it begets media. This is about your press release thing. I booked myself for a radio show – not anything crazy, a nice market on the west coast, kind of a personal development-type radio show, who knows how many people are listening, but I haven't done a radio show in a while so I want to do it. It's a good fit into one of my books and I can talk about it and give a good interview, so we're going to do it.

You hear people say, "Send those people a press release!" All I said was, I looked at their show, it took me two minutes to go to their website, I saw the recent few topics, saw the kind of show they do, and I sent them a title and a subject line. I think it was Tom and Rich who were the hosts. I said, "Tom and Rich, here's a show topic idea for you," blah blah blah. "By the way, my name's Mike Dolpies. I'm the author of this book, and I'd love to help your audience," *yada, yada, yada.* "By the way, here's two clips of two recent television appearances so you can get to know me."

They contacted me back within 20 minutes and said, "Hey, can we book you for Friday?" You'd think, "Hey, you need to send those people a press release to get on their show," and I was a radio show host with a weekly show in a weekly market. People sent me press releases, and that's not how you book. I never booked anybody by those press releases.

First, I booked my friends, then I booked my networking partners, and after they were all gone, then I booked people that had ideas for me. [laughing]

BEN SETTLE: Would you have gotten that opportunity if you didn't have those two TV interviews to send them, though?

MIKE DOLPIES: Maybe, maybe not, but here's what I would have done. I wouldn't have been so arrogant. [laughing] Those two TV interviews made me more arrogant about it, and I was able to use more of a take-away sell. "Eh, if you want it, great. If not, I don't really care, man." That was kind of my approach. I didn't say it in my email, but that was the tone of my email.

Here's how I got radio show interviews before I had TV interviews, and it was the radio interviews that helped me get more TV interviews. It's like a professional cycle here. If I wasn't able to throw those links, what I would do is I would just blow out my topic a little more and make it more compelling. That's called a pitch, and this again goes to what you said, instead of press releases.

I'd do the same thing. "Tom and Rich, here's a good show segment idea." You're in business and you need to – especially if they're reading your stuff, they understand the power of words applied to this. This goes back to my 60/40 thing. You're already doing 60% of this. You need to tweak it to the other 40%. If you're studying marketing, you're studying copywriting, you're studying email marketing, and you're in tune with the Ben Settle doctrine, you already know the power of words.

BEN SETTLE: God help you! But go ahead. [laughing]

MIKE DOLPIES: Basically what I'd do is I'd take the same thing, and I wouldn't start out with, "My name's Mike and I'm the author of the book..." – I would make my pitch lead into, "This would be a great segment. Here's what we would cover," and I'd hit some bullet points of what we would cover.

Then I would say, "My name is Mike. I'm the author of this book," with a short little bio and a link to my book. Done. That works when you don't have anything behind you. Now you have to say, "How can I get my foot in the door by giving them such a compelling pitch" – it's a pitch, not a press release.

Subject line first: Tom and Rich, here's a great show idea.

You blow out the idea, or maybe you say the problem, like procrastination, blah blah blah. It kills a lot of dreams and it keeps people fat, or whatever your subject line is, if you're using procrastination. Then you hit the bullet points, "Here's what I would cover. Let's book this asap, because Procrastination Week is coming up," or whatever. This is not exactly how it unfolded yesterday, but I'm just giving an example when you don't have anything behind you. You have to now think of pitches of how your topic ties in.

Like you're big on email marketing. Where does that tie in right now? It ties in because like in *The Wall Street Journal* last week, "Will Facebook Email Kill Email Marketing?"

BEN SETTLE: Yeah, that's a boon for people like me right now to talk about that.

MIKE DOLPIES: Yeah, because that was in *The Wall Street Journal.*

BEN SETTLE: You know what, I wrote that subject line almost a year ago actually, that exact subject line. [laughing]

MIKE DOLPIES: [inaudible] either know or you don't know. *The Wall Street Journal* yesterday was about how Facebook is actually going to be offering an @Facebook.com email address. That's what's different now.

Facebook messages, yes, I hear what you're saying there. They've been around since Facebook started, but now Facebook is offering a new service, which gives you an @Facebook.com email address, so it's going to be BenSettle@Facebook.com. Don't email him there, he doesn't have the account, but BenSettle@Facebook.com. That's going to be an email account that stores all your social media, all your Facebook messages and whatever else you've got going on, all the things from your ex-girlfriend, and all your other emails. Then it actually has a spot for newsletters and stuff that's not a priority. As an email marketing expert, there's a lot of companies right now that are really ramping up their email. If you study big retailers, the smart ones – Walgreen's, Best Buy – they have great email marketing. To your standards they don't have great email marketing, but to big company standards they're aggressive with their email marketing.

So, for someone like *The Wall Street Journal* or say Fox Business News type thing, you might have something there. "Email expert speaks – Will Facebook email destroy email marketing and hurt our economy more?"

I'm just throwing things out there, but you see where I'm going with this?

BEN SETTLE: Yeah, I do. That's very interesting.

MIKE DOLPIES: This is how I think.

BEN SETTLE: Now I'm going to ask you this. Do you recommend people email their pitches and not call or mail, but email first?

MIKE DOLPIES: What a funny irony. Yes, you email your pitches, absolutely. It's still a major form of communication. If you find out the producer or the person with the show or the editor has an @Facebook email address, fire away to that @Facebook email address. Send them a Facebook message if you want.

BEN SETTLE: I shouldn't say this, because we'll say email and a few over-zealous whippersnappers will go, "I'm going to get a big list, import it, and mass mail."

MIKE DOLPIES: No, no broadcast email here. Everything is personal if you want it to work. So, Tom and Rich got one email. Call me old-fashioned if you want. Call me someone who's not leveraging my time right, because I have a broadcast email system, but I only email Tom and Rich.

Man, what a sin I just committed because I didn't email 1,000 Tom and Rich's. No! That's the only show that it ties into.

If I emailed you, Ben, you have The Ben Settle Show. If I emailed you with the topic I emailed Tom and Rich, you're going to go like, "Dude, that doesn't fit for what my people want. What's the matter with you? Are you sick today? Is there something wrong? Can I help you in any way?" That's how you're going to think. Again, it's all customized to the outlet. That's the thing you've got to remember, and that's where the pitches come in. Steve Jobs can send a press release out about the new iPad. Big companies can do that. Wendy's can say, "Hey, we're changing the recipe of our French fries," and unfortunately for us as the general public, we're going to have to watch that if we're watching the news. "Great. Wendy's changing the recipe."

They can send out press releases to these massive lists that they have, because they're big companies. As a small-time operator, you can't do that because nobody cares if your local burger joint is changing their fries recipe. They don't give a rat's behind, but Wendy's can do that.

It sucks, but it's true. It happens. Big companies can send press releases. Big CEOs can send press releases. Bill Clinton's PR people can send a press release out that says, "Bill Clinton is now going on a vegan diet," – by the way, it was news about three months ago, just so you know that – but we can't. The vast majority of people can't do that. Does that make sense?

BEN SETTLE: I just find this very fascinating, because I kind of came of age in PR doing the Hartunian system, and yours is vastly different. It's interesting because I don't see either one as necessarily being better than the other, but this is a great other way to do it if you don't want to screw around with faxing out press releases.

MIKE DOLPIES: Yeah, I don't know, I won't say because I haven't done it. Here's what happened. I looked at that same approach and maybe I got stuck on the technology. I couldn't find a good broadcast fax.

Then I also knew that the more personal I could make this, the better. It's Tom and Rich. That's what I knew, and a lot of my mentors as well also mentioned that. Target one at a time, and then let them call you. That's the approach on this, by the way. Target one at a time as you go, and then as you build up this huge bank, then you let your media start to work for you. Here's an example. I got Entrepreneur magazine only because my local state business publication puts out articles in print that I give them, and they maybe do one or two a month, because it only comes out twice a month in publication. They do maybe 24-26 issues a year. I don't know what their exact publication schedule is.

That's how I got Entrepreneur.com. You've already built a relationship with the local people, and now all the sudden Entrepreneur picked that up, so I didn't have to go pitch Entrepreneur. Does that make sense?

BEN SETTLE: Yeah. What I find very interesting about this is if somebody really wanted to go balls out with PR, honestly, if I had more time I think I would actually do this, if I had more of a mass market I was selling to than who I sell to –

MIKE DOLPIES: Ben, you just gave me the email pitch.

BEN SETTLE: You could do both. There's this one guy, he sells special effects cookbooks. He gets on the Food Network all the time, and he does the Hartunian thing. He doesn't fax, he just snail mails. He'll send out like ten a day, and you can do that. At the same time you can do the targeting that you're talking about. You can do the shotgun approach to everybody, and then do your targeting thing with email, and you could really clean up.

MIKE DOLPIES: I can't knock the shotgun approach because it's not something that I've embraced and I've actually said, "Okay, this doesn't work," but I'll tell you what, here's what doesn't work. Press releases to the targeting approach doesn't work. It's a weird irony, isn't it?

If you actually do a press release and you target it personally, that hurts your chances. It doesn't kill them, but it hurts them.

BEN SETTLE: It's kind of a waste of time.

MIKE DOLPIES: It's a weird thing. You do the whole press release – For Immediate Release – Contact yada yada yada, your headline and all this kind of stuff – I know how to write press releases and I've written some that I've picked up for clients too, but then on a targeted or personal approach, that actually doesn't work.

When it comes to local media, maybe like for you, you would fit really good into your state business publications. You would fit good into that. Some of your stuff I've read kind of has a personal development flair in a way. I've read some of your emails, which could easily be turned into articles, so you have some stuff that does have some broad appeal. You could probably do an article for a local newspaper if you really worked at it and if you wanted to do it. You could do one for a local business publication. You'd fit in there perfectly.

And I think if you had your radar or your antenna up, now all the sudden you see that Facebook email made *The Wall Street Journal* and *USA Today*, and now your head starts to spin like, "How am I going to tie into this as an email marketing expert?" and there you go. Now you're hitting your email marketing topic to a huge audience.

There's a percentage of people who read *The Wall Street Journal* and *USA Today* that are interested in email marketing for sure. If they hear from an email marketing expert who's got something to say – and you know Fox News is owned by the same company *The Wall Street Journal* is, so there's an interview on Fox News. I'm just painting this picture for you. I'm not saying it's guaranteed, but it's just an example of how you work it. This is your subject, so you have your local stuff that you're doing that's evergreen. It doesn't rely on, "Hey, Facebook came out with their new email service." That's something you would pounce on right away.

I usually jump on stupid goofy weeks, like the last TV segment I did was "How to beat a path to your door week." I do internet marketing, so I said one of the best ways to get people to beat a path to your door is to have a good internet marketing strategy. That was my whole segment. The pitch was a lot better than that, but pretty much that was it, to sum it up. Does that make sense?

BEN SETTLE: Yeah. This kind of goes along with another question I was going to ask you. Somebody who's reading this or listening to this, whatever they're selling, they just need to keep aware of what the mass media is talking about. If they can tie something in, that's a perfect opportunity for them to do what you're teaching here.

MIKE DOLPIES: Yeah, and two examples. I have a lot of martial arts guys, and bullying is something that's on the national radar screen, so I've had a few of them that it's a slam dunk for them to get local segments or get articles or get the newspaper to come out and cover their anti-bully seminar.

The other side is you look at your evergreen. If you write an article for a publication, I've got a couple clients on my roster right now that came because of articles in the rinky-dinkiest papers, and then I have other ones that came from trade journals, a couple other ones that came from like state business publications, so writing articles is one way to get publicity. We can talk about that if you want for a few minutes.

The other side of it is you have your kind of evergreen publicity strategy. For me, the next thing on my radar screen is New Year's resolutions. We're recording this the week of Thanksgiving, but the next thing on my radar screen is New Year's resolutions. I know that I'll be contacting producers and saying, "Here's a segment idea for New Year's resolutions." Obviously, it's going to be a lot better than, and sound better than that. It's going to be a sound bite if you think about it, and hopefully they'll say, "Great. Let's book you for December 27." So, you have your evergreen strategy that doesn't tie into anything, and then, like you were saying, you jump on other things. With you, we used the Facebook email example because you're an email marketing expert, and that would tie into business-type publications like *The Wall Street Journal, USA Today,* or Fox Business Channel or CNBC might cover that.

BEN SETTLE: Let me ask you this, and you only have five minutes to answer, so I'm putting you on the super-hot seat. You talked about writing articles and doing your own radio show. Somebody could take maybe articles they've already written for the internet and they could turn that into an article – they've already done most of the work – and they could submit it. How does that work? How do they get into these publications?

MIKE DOLPIES: Sometimes, some of us that put articles out there on the internet, it's kind of like the tree falling in the forest, to a point. So a lot of times you probably aren't going to worry too much about it. There are some magazines that are really sticklers about they want first priority for it, so you've got to check on that. It's not just about recycling your stuff, so you've got to be careful. You may want to tweak at first, and you may want to do some independent research whether they want first priority. Just call them as Joe Schmoe and ask the question. Say, "For freelance articles, is it really important that this is the first place it appears?"

Most times, if you get someone on the phone they'll answer the question, or use a different email address or something like that. If they don't get back to you, great. Just draw the conclusion it's better if they get it first. A state magazine or a local state business publication or newspaper, or even a big outlet – which obviously this doesn't apply to Entrepreneur, because it appeared in print before it appeared on their website – but for most of them, assume that they want first dibs on it.

You could basically take articles and you can do two things. How I got my first article to appear in a local business publication, and then after that on a regular basis, it was funny. I interviewed the editor on my radio show first, so that was my in. I said, "Hey Bob, you want to come on my radio show and talk about your newspaper?" and we did a segment that highlighted his newspaper. He was happy about that. He was getting a little media exposure. Then maybe about a month later I had this article that I wrote, and I was going to either put it on my blog or throw it out there somewhere, so I said, "Let me ask Bob."

I sent Bob an email that said, "Bob, here's a good article idea for you," and I put the nice catchy title in there. "This would be great for this time of year because the New Year is coming and we need to get business owners moving," or something like that. I forget what I put. He said, "Sure, send it over. Make sure it's between 600-750 words." So, I went and looked at it, it's between 600-750 words, and I said, "Oh, by the way, this hasn't appeared anywhere else. Let me know if you like it." He said, "Great, I like it. We're going to run it January 10." Done.

That's how you do it. You look at what they publish and then you offer them something. Four or five years ago I got my first article to appear in a martial arts industry trade magazine. I read the magazine religiously every month for like six years, and then I realized I was really good at selling martial arts. That's what I loved to do – enroll students, talk to their parents, enroll them as adults or whatever, and get them started in the school. That's what I enjoyed. I noticed, "You know, there's no darn column in this magazine about enrolling people." Duh. It's only like one of the lifebloods of our business. So, I emailed the editor and I emailed the president of the trade association and said, "Hey, you guys need an article on selling. Here's a few ideas," and they were like, "All right, you're on, cowboy."

So, I started writing an article for them every month until the magazine changed hands. The new owners didn't like me, so they canned my column. Anyway, not to get off on a tangent, but does that answer your question?

BEN SETTLE: Yeah. I think this is very interesting. To wind this down, you've created a special course on how to get local publicity. What's in that, and what's that all about?

MIKE DOLPIES: It's *7 Day Local Celebrity.* It's got four hours of audio and then the transcript. Everything else that you have on your mind right now, it answers all those questions.

It basically takes someone from total newbie, and it digs deeper into what you said. You kind of said, "Wait a minute, if you're not on TV, then what do you do? How do you get your own radio show?" and it covers all that – all the way from how to get your own radio show, your own real TV show if you want to do it locally, how to wheel and deal and make that happen, and then like I said how to get on your local network affiliates, how to draft a pitch – really, all the in's and out's and all the details of crafting a pitch.

There's a couple pitch examples you can send to local editors or radio producers, and just a lot of strategy. Doberman Dan is the one who did the interviews, and he pulled all the information out of me. It took us almost four hours.

You just absorb the material and you're kind of like downloading everything that we talked about here, but even more so, because you're getting the whole thing. You can literally be up and running in seven days – have your first pitches crafted, have your targets, who you're going to go after, and literally start getting publicity very quickly. That's really what the program covers.

BEN SETTLE: Mike, I can't tell you how cool this conversation has been. I've been wanting to ask you about this forever, and I'm glad that you agreed to do this. Thank you.

Bonus Supplement to Using the Media from the October 2011 Issue of "Email Players"

Yes, I speaketh of using email (free, fast and "low impact" email) to get your righteous self-booked on radio shows, TV shows, and in magazines, newspapers and other prestigious publications. This can jump start your website traffic (if you get in a big enough show or publication) and sales like nothing you've experienced. But, even MORE important than the money and traffic and financial benefits is this: **There is NO better way to give yourself instant credibility, celebrity-appeal and, yes, "expert status" than getting in the media!** (And think about using THOSE credentials in the David Dutton email -- "I was on TV recently talking about..." In fact, one reason I now have a "media" page on my site is to position myself FAR above the other email ex-spurts out there (there are MANY wannabes out there) so people feel "safe" opting in. And the media is doing that for me without it costing me one red cent. In fact, just last week I nabbed two radio show interviews (real radio shows on real radio stations -- not podcasts, although podcasts in your niche are list-building GOLDMINES, and you can use this exact same technique I'm going to show you to get podcast interviews, too) with essentially the same email. And I'm going to continue to KEEP using this same email (which I'm about to show you) to get booked on shows for the foreseeable future. After all, this is building my list with people I'd NEVER reach otherwise. Plus, at the same time, it's giving me celebrity status. We are (like it or lump it) in what publicity expert Paul Hartunian calls a "celebrity obsessed" culture. Nobody cares what "experts" think anymore. That's why some Hollywood airhead can write an error-filled book on a serious medical subject and get on all the big talk shows and sell millions of copies... while the "for real" medical experts (who are not celebrities) toil away begging for grant money and funding. It's sad, but that's the way it is. And by properly using the media, you can get that celebrity status AND have your expert status -- **making you virtually impervious to being knocked off by your competition**. All of which will help you build your list, attract (or approach) JV partners, etc.

Okay, enough build up. Here's what we're gonna do: First, I'm going to give you the method behind my madness. I'm going to tell you exactly HOW to get on radio shows using email (it's very easy). Then, I'm going to show you the emails I sent out last week to get booked on radio. All you have to do is follow my instructions and use the emails as templates (literally swap out my info with yours). In addition, did you notice the golden-rod paper transcript enclosed with this issue? That is an interview I did with Mike Dolpies who showed me how to do this. And it goes into even MORE detail (he's the real expert on this) on how this works. But in the meantime, let's talk about getting you in the media. First off, what you want to do is go to this website -- www.RadioGuestList.com -- and sign up for their media alerts. (There are other sites too, but just start with this one). What will happen is, you will get alerted regularly about media reporters and talk show hosts looking for experts to interview. Depending on what you sell, you will see a lot of them (just check through their site archives under your category) or maybe just a few. But chances are whatever you sell, you can find a show that fits your topic. And then, when you see one that fits your product/service/business you send this EXACT email (but with your details, of course) to the contact person. It's so easy, the alerts even tell you exactly who to contact -- via email -- for each show!

Subject Line: Re: The Next Level hosted by Anthony Gemma

Rebecca,

I saw your listing today on Radioguestlist.com.

Here's a quick segment idea for "The Next Level" hosted by Anthony Gemma:

"How to use email to become
a celebrity and leader
in your industry"

One of the best ways any business can thrive during bad economies is to position themselves as both a celebrity and a leader in their industry. One of the fastest and cheapest ways to do that is with email. And by using just a few proven email marketing principles, your listeners can easily position themselves as the only choice for their customers and leads to buy from.

Here are some talking points I can share:

• How some of the most successful and respected companies on the planet use the "F Word" in their email marketing to get top marketplace positioning
• Why being an expert is not enough anymore to be trusted by today's

skeptical customers

• How to write emails customers love to read and buy from in just 10-15 minutes (works especially well for people who hate writing)

About...

Ben Settle is a web entrepreneur and email marketing specialist. He is the author of "The Email Player's Cookbook" and "Street-Smart Email", and he publishes daily email marketing tips on his website at www.BenSettle.com. His clients have included everyone from small start-ups on "shoe string budgets" to prestigious companies earning over $20 million per year.

Email: ben@bensettle.com
Phone: ###-###-####

Now, I'm always tweaking this. That was the first one I sent out. It nabbed me an interview a day or so later. But here's the second one I used, slightly tweaked -- where I spaced out the bullets, used different "About" verbiage, shortened it etc. Again, I'm always improving this as I go. You don't have to get it perfect, just get it written...

Subject Line: Re: The Toldedo Biz Talk Radio Show

Cindy,

I saw your listing today on Radioguestlist.com.

Here's a quick segment idea for "The Toledo Biz Talk Radio Show":

"How to write simple emails
your customers will love
reading and buying from"

Here are some talking points I can share:

• How to write emails customers look forward to reading and buying from

• A very simple email secret (seen in "Dear Abby" columns) a few, very savvy businesses use to sell millions of dollars worth of products online each year

• Why using spellcheck can make your emails less profitable

About...

Ben Settle is an email marketing specialist and editor of "The Email Players Newsletter". He is also the author of "The Email Player's Cookbook" and "Street-Smart Email", and publishes daily email marketing tips on his website at www.BenSettle.com. His clients have included everyone from small start-ups on "shoe string budgets" to prestigious companies earning over $20 million per year.

Email: ben@bensettle.com
Phone: ###-###-####

And finally, just so you know this template works over and over and over... just now (as I'm writing this issue!) a new show alert came through RadioGuestList.com. Here's what I just dashed out:

Barbara,

I saw your listing today on Radioguestlist.com.

Here's a quick segment idea for "Monday Nights for You- A to Z Business":

"How to Use Simple Little Emails to
Double Your Sales in a Bad Economy"

Here are some talking points I can share:

• How to use email to generate a surge of new sales in 24 hours or less (perfect for businesses needing quick cash flow)

• A neurological discovery that makes it super easy to quickly create profitable emails (works especially well for people who hate writing)

• The "talk radio" secret of writing emails customers love reading and buying from

• The case against making emails look professional or fancy

About...

Ben Settle is one of the world's leading email marketing specialists, and editor of the prestigious "Email Players" newsletter. He is also the author of "The Email Player's Cookbook" and "Street-Smart Email", and publishes daily email marketing tips on his website at www.BenSettle.com. His clients have included everyone from small start-ups on "shoe string budgets" to independent entrepreneurs earning over $20 million per year.

Email: ben@bensettle.com
Phone: ###-###-####

So, there you have it. Three emails showing you <u>exactly</u> how to do this. Plus, it doesn't have to take you more than 3 minutes. What I do is, I have a master list of bullets (talking points) and themes saved on my computer. Whenever a show alert comes through, I simply look at the show description, pick a theme that I think will work and fill in the template with that theme and a few different talking points. This makes it very simple and fast. Plus, I'm probably the <u>first</u> person to respond to these alerts, which gives me tremendous leverage. Again, check out the enclosed interview with this issue for even more details on how to do this. It's the same basic template each time. And you can easily adapt it for your business and use RadioGuestList.com to start booking yourself on shows. This can not only potentially build your email list (quickly), but it can give you the kind of rock-solid credibility most (if not all) of your competitors won't be able to touch with a 10-foot pole. And again, I already mentioned this, but you can use the email format above to get interview for podcasts in your niche. I'm finding radio is great for credibility and the "halo effect" but podcasts with people in my niche are way better for building a list of people who come to your site wanting to opt in. You still can get people on your list from radio shows, but so far (and this may just be my situation) podcasts are much better. But that credibility you get from being on real radio shows gives you a leg up when wanting to get the attention of podcasters and/or JV partners. Just something to think about...

Chapter 7
Simple List Building Secrets
of a "Fringe" Traffic Scientist
Google Loooooves
Giving Oodles of Traffic to

BEN SETTLE: I'm talking to my friend, Jim Yaghi, who's a computer scientist. I call what he does "fringe marketing" because he really is on the fringe of scientific traffic generation. Once upon a time last year he taught me about a way to use SEO without having to do any tricks or anything. It's completely Google-proof because Google wants you to do this, so they'll never not want you to do this, as far as we know at least, unless Google has a complete meltdown or becomes run by morons or something. They want you to do this. This is a Google-proof way. I've done it back when I was running this other site for the male health industry, and I did remember getting significantly more searches and people finding my site doing this. I'm going to shut up now and, Jim, I want to thank you for being here, first of all.

JIM YAGHI: Thank you, Ben. When I was growing up, it was not cool to be a computer scientist.

BEN SETTLE: You probably got stuffed in a locker for being a computer scientist.

JIM YAGHI: It was so not cool, and nowadays you can say, "This guy's a computer scientist," and suddenly everybody's like, "Oh, okay. What does he have to say, because he must know what he's talking about." It's funny how these things change. As far as this method is concerned, Ben, your Email Players are going to be listening to this, right? These guys will hopefully be the kind of people who don't mind writing emails and are constantly looking for new writing ideas, so this is a really good method for you guys. Most of the people who I've encountered who do SEO actually don't like this technique because it requires you to create content, to write stuff, useful stuff, but the advantage here is not just traffic. Did you notice, Ben, that when you did this technique, what you got was also targeted traffic who were actually prepared to buy?

BEN SETTLE: Yeah, it was definitely a higher-quality lead, there's no question about it.

JIM YAGHI: Most of the SEO techniques that people are using are done in such a way that they attract all kinds of generic audiences almost. I mean they get the keyword ranking in the search engine, they get to the top of that particular search that they're trying to get to, but then the traffic they end up attracting is almost strays and stragglers, outliers almost. You get a lot of leads come through from third-world countries that are not really likely to be buyers anyway. They're probably scraping for content or something like that. You get a lot of bot searches come through. You might see a spike in your traffic, but it's just mainly bot traffic and not real. You put out garbage – and essentially that's what they're doing, they're putting out garbage – and you're going to get garbage. Most of the SEO'ers who use those techniques, at face value it looks like they're doing very well. They're getting their site ranked, so the metrics are all good, they're tip-top, but then you look at what the actual results say and they're benefiting a very small fraction from that traffic. They only benefit a little bit from it. You've got to generate 1,000 hits to make use of like 10. That's kind of the numbers that you see, and it's really hard work. You've seen those guys, right Ben, who do the traditional SEO?

BEN SETTLE: Dude, I was doing that stuff because a mutual person we know was into this, and it's fine. It wasn't like it was bad. It was working at the time, because this was before Google started penalizing all the article sites. Then after that it stopped working, all that traditional stuff, at least for me. Then you taught me this thing and it kept me going. It kept me in the game when everybody else was falling out.

JIM YAGHI: Totally, yeah. The main thing that sets this apart that makes it "Google-proof" is that it's a method that gives Google what it actually wants from its content creators. It just gives them exactly what they want. They want good-quality content, they want useful content, they want it to be targeted to the intent of the people who are searching, and that's essentially what we end up giving them. The method is really simple. Do you want me to give an overview of the method and then talk about the differences, or should we start with the differences?

BEN SETTLE: However you think is the best way to teach it. I know it's really simple, but I know there are some moving parts there, so whatever makes sense to you. I'm the student here, man. I'm learning from you again, so however you want to do it.

JIM YAGHI: I always introduce it like this, Ben, because I need to show you what's wrong with the other method and how this solves what's wrong with it. What most SEO people do is they'll pick out a search keyword that they believe their website should rank for. Say they have a chiropractor's website, so they'll go and try to target something like *Glendora chiropractor.* They decide – and in this case, it's probably not far from the truth – that *Glendora chiropractor* is a very targeted search term that people who want a chiropractor in their area are going to search for. If they find them at the top of that search, then they're going to want to give their business to this person, or they're more likely to give their person whose website is showing first. So, they pick this keyword, *Glendora chiropractor,* and they go and they now start to do all these things, engineering Google to give them that top placement. They start by creating keyword-stuffed articles where they take *Glendora chiropractor* and insert it as many times as they can into the articles and into their website in such a way that it's so frequent that it doesn't even read naturally anymore.

I don't know if you've ever read people's content who seem to be really concerned with SEO.

BEN SETTLE: Yeah, they repeat certain phrases and it's very weird-sounding.

JIM YAGHI: It sounds awful. Maybe to the untrained eye it's not immediately obvious what they're trying to do, but I know a big marketer who's very much into his SEO, and he likes to blog and be creative with his blog posts, and these two things don't seem to work very well together.

If you want to be creative and do SEO, you're kind of bumping your head against the wall because traditional SEO has all these rules for how many times a phrase should be repeated. This exact phrase has to be repeated several times, and you have to have some variations on it, and blah blah blah – all these weird crazy rules. So, you're sitting there having your creativity stumped by the fact that you're trying to repeat this phrase so many times in all the right places, and that's just part of the equation they have to do. On top of that they're always looking at addressing the symptom rather than the cause, so they will constantly do it the wrong way around. Now they've created the content or the article with the header tags and the body and all these strict rules about how many times a phrase should be repeated, and then they take that article and they spin it now. Spinning is because they know the search engines "penalize" duplicate content, so they'll take the article and create a variation of it by changing certain words around, like using synonyms and stuff like that. They'll just go through, and there's usually scripts that allow them to spin the article into an article that cosmetically looks different, but is still essentially the same material. There's just some words changed around for a synonym. I don't know if you've ever seen content like that, but I see it all the time.

BEN SETTLE: Definitely. In fact, I see it more now than I used to, which is kind of strange.

JIM YAGHI: It's like these weird replacement words that they put in place. It's obviously done by somebody who doesn't know English very well or something.

BEN SETTLE: Right, that's exactly what it's like.

JIM YAGHI: These programs are looking up words in a thesaurus, like all these automated tools to get SEO. They're looking up a word in a thesaurus and they're putting in a synonym, which is not necessarily the best replacement word in this context. Now that we've talked about these spun articles, why do they do that? Because they're going to take that article in all the different variations and put it on all these different websites all over the internet. Then they start their backlink building process, which is essentially giving authority to their useless garbage content stuffed with keywords that has been spun by what sounds like a non-native speaker who's written it. Now they want to give authority to it by boosting the number of sites that are linking back into it. They'll try to find sites that have some kind of authority. Authority is just a relative term that the search engines use to classify a website as, "Okay, this tends to have authoritative information. It's a resource website. It's a useful site." Wikipedia, for example, is a high-authority website. If you get a link back from Wikipedia to your website, it's like you're rubbing shoulders with Richard Branson. If you're friends with Richard Branson, some of his authority will seep through to you in other people's eyes. If Ben Settle is a respected email specialist and he's friends with Jim Yaghi, then Jim Yaghi kind of gets a little bit of authority from that. I'm not an email specialist by any means, but lately I've been getting people contacting me and asking me to give them interviews on email writing.

BEN SETTLE: I've sent a couple of those guys to you. [laughing]

JIM YAGHI: [laughing] That's cool, but the point is I'm not an email specialist, or I'm not branded as an email specialist, and some of your authority is seeping through to me just because of the fact that we know each other. In the same way, these people are trying to get links back from websites that have authority so that will give themselves a false authority, because it's not real. It's not earned.

So what is wrong with all of this? What's wrong, Ben, is that it's not natural, it's all forced. Everything about it is forced, from A to Z. The choice of keyword that they picked is forced. That's not necessarily a keyword that people are actually looking for, even though it might turn up in a keyword search tool. *Glendora chiropractor –*

maybe there's some people searching for it, but that's not a natural search that every single person who's interested in finding a chiropractor in their neighborhood is going to be looking for. The content that they used is forced. It's not really genuinely relevant content, because you don't really know that this is what somebody wants when they type *Glendora chiropractor* – that they're looking for a chiropractor in Glendora that they can go and get treated with. They may be looking for chiropractors in Glendora because they'd like to market to them, right? They're trying to compile a database of all the different chiropractors in Glendora so they can market to them. Maybe their SEO is scoping out the competition. There's all kinds of intents behind a search like that, so it's not actually a natural search or a natural relevance that they're finding this particular website or content.

The content itself has been bastardized into something disgusting, spun rubbish that looks like a computer spat it out, which is exactly what it is. The backlinks from all sorts of websites are not authentic. It's not somebody who genuinely believes that this content is authoritative, and then went and linked to it in Wikipedia. You see those references at the bottom of a Wikipedia article? Those are authorities. When a Wikipedia writer goes and uses a website as a source in creating the content for that Wikipedia article, the link that they put in there as a reference to that site, which could be your site if you're SEO optimizing, that link is a natural authoritative link because they have actually seen value in this. It's kind of like the difference between somebody who forces himself into Richard Branson's circle so that he can seem authoritative when he has no knowledge about business, is a useless f*ck who managed to weasel his way into Branson's circle to take a fictitious photograph next to him, who snuck into a photo or something like that to try to make people believe that he really is part of Branson's circle, when in reality he's not. That's the difference between him and somebody who Branson genuinely likes and does business with or is friends with and respects. That's real authority.

All of this goes against what Google wants from the web. They're actually constantly changing their algorithms and improving them so that they can get rid of people like that, because these artificial SEO results are not what they're looking for. People are not happy when they arrive on these websites. If they're featured in the Google search, they actually damage the Google search's reputation. If they come up on the Google search and somebody lands on it and they're like, "What the hell is this? What is this content? I can't even understand or make heads or tails of this thing. It sounds like it's spat out of a machine," it will damage Google's reputation, so Google is constantly trying to kill off that content, making it more difficult for them to actually engineer and SEO-optimize.

That's where our method – the reverse SEO method – doesn't suffer the same problems. The way that it works is in the opposite way. That's why it's called reverse SEO. Everything about it is organic and natural. Here are the instructions for making use of this method for your Email Players – you lucky people, you. What you do is you go and you write your article or emails or whatever, relevant content to your audience as you see fit. Be creative, write your content, answer questions, think of various problems that people in your industry have, go look at forums and see what people are asking and answer some of those questions, and so on and so forth. Just go out and be creative and post content. Before you do that, there's one thing that you need to make sure that you're doing. Make sure that you have Google Analytics installed on your site. If you use WordPress, which I think a lot of you do – right, Ben?

BEN SETTLE: Oh yeah, I think that's pretty much standard for most people that I'm dealing with at least.

JIM YAGHI: Awesome. If you're using WordPress, then you'll find a plugin for Google Analytics. Make sure it's installed and running correctly and start looking at your stats back there to make sure that it's correctly working. Google Analytics, for those of you who are not too familiar with it, gives you statistics on your website use – how people discover your site, where they come from, which other websites refer them, what search keywords they use, what the demographics of the audience are, where they're located in geography of the world, what kind of browser they're using, if they're on a mobile device or desktop computer, and all kinds of information like that. There's all sorts of info. It's a very, very useful tool. A lot of people find it so big and complicated that they don't bother to install it, and that's the biggest worst mistake. Even if you don't plan to do anything with it, make sure you install it because somebody's going to come along one of these days. You might hire someone to help you out with traffic or something like that, and the data that it would have collected and stored for you is priceless, so make sure that you have that installed. It's one-click install and simple. Go to www.analytics.google.com and set up an account there. Just associate it with your Gmail or whatever. Then take the ID number that they give you there, because they give you some code that you can copy and paste to your pages. It's just a small ID number in there. Grab that and just paste it into the Analytics plugin on WordPress. Once you've got that going, then you can start posting content. Before you start to see any keywords turn up – which is what we're looking for, and I'll explain in a second – you'll need to start posting articles at least once a day for probably around two weeks, give or take, depending on the traffic and all that, before you can start to expect to see some of the data that we're looking for now.

BEN SETTLE: How many articles do you recommend? Just one a day for 14 days, or as many as you can?

JIM YAGHI: As many as you can, but 14 articles is good. Make sure they're good high-quality articles directed at your audience with the intent of selling something.

BEN SETTLE: Does it have to be a hard word count of at least 500 words, in your opinion?

JIM YAGHI: Not at all. How many weeks did it take before you started seeing the keywords show up at first?

BEN SETTLE: This was like two years ago so I don't remember, but it didn't seem like it was that long. Two weeks is probably about what it took, just going on memory. It didn't take real long. I would start seeing stuff within a few days for one or two keywords. I see what you're saying with 14 days before you can really start getting a lot of different keywords.

JIM YAGHI: My wife just did the exercise recently and it took her about two weeks before she started to see it. She just told me now that it took her two weeks. She was posting daily, so 14 articles essentially. They weren't very long articles. They don't have to be. Just make sure that they're good articles, kind of like the emails that we write.

BEN SETTLE: But maybe a little bit more meat?

JIM YAGHI: Sure. It doesn't really matter, honestly. What I highly recommend – and this is just part of strategy; it's not necessarily a requirement for the technique to work, but strategy-wise – do question/answer type content, at least for those days, because it's a little bit more effective in getting you to that place you need to be. What we're looking for is for keywords to begin to show up in Google Analytics. Keywords are the search strings that people are searching for on Google and then discovering your site in Google. You've got to make sure your site is indexed too, by the way. Once it starts to show up in the Google index when someone runs a search, that is what we want to know. We want to know what are the actual searches that people have run in order to discover our site. I'm going to pull it up here and find it, just so I can tell you exactly where to find it. When you sign into your account on analytics.google.com, you're going to see your general overview screen, or before that you'll see the different accounts you have, if you have more than one. Open up the site that you're tracking and then you'll see the main audience overview screen. What you want to do here, before anything else, is make sure that you set the date range in the top right as far back as the history of the website and as far forward as the site has existed. For example, my site has been around since I think 2009, so I'll put 2009 at the very beginning as the beginning of the date range. Then for the final date range we'll just put today's date in there. What that will do is show you all the stats for the entire period that your site has been in existence.

The next thing to do is in the Traffic Sources tab on the left, click there and you're going to get another menu. You want to click on Sources, then Search, then Organic. Once you've done that you're going to get a list of all the search queries that have ever been used to discover your site, ever since of course you've had Analytics installed. If you're lucky enough to have installed Analytics from before, you should already see some keywords in there. If not, no biggie. You'll start to see some things show up there. I want to make a small distinction here between the phrase *search query* and *keyword* or *search keyword*. A search query, unlike a search keyword, is the actual search string – the actual thing that a person typed into a search box – when they were looking for something. That will tend to be a long specific query, like I'm seeing here a search query that says *why put bid on ppc.* That's an actual search query. You'll see prepositions in there and things like that, which will kind of giveaway that it's an actual search query. Search keywords should not be confused with a search query. A keyword is more of a technical term. A search query is from a user standpoint. What did they type into the search? A keyword, on the other hand, is kind of a unifying version of multiple search queries that are similar, and then you end up with a representative phrase that looks like a search query, but it's not a search query because it actually represents a range of search queries. I guess I'm confusing things, Ben. If this is confusing, can you ask me questions that will make it more clear?

BEN SETTLE: It's not that confusing because, honestly, at the end of the day, even if they don't understand this or I don't understand it, the how-to of this is pretty simple. You're just giving the overview here, like why this works. If it goes over someone's head, they need to get off Facebook for a few minutes and think and they'll be all right. I'm not worried about it. It's good.

JIM YAGHI: Okay. The keywords that people see, they usually pull up from a keyword tool like the Google keyword tool. The Google keyword tool will give you all these stats and it looks like, "Oh, there's lots of people searching for *online marketing success,*" but *online marketing success* essentially represents a range of different search queries that kind of mean *online marketing success.* Maybe a question like *how can I get success in online marketing* will be lumped together with *online marketing success* and you'll see the volume of searches and competition and blah

blah blah show up over there. We're not concerned with any of that stuff. I don't really care about the keyword. What I care about is the search query. What did somebody type into a search box and find my website? What was the actual search they ran? What we're seeing here in this view is the actual search queries, exactly what people had typed into a search box in order to discover your site. What's interesting about this is that you'll not see a search string in here unless somebody had typed it, hit Enter, saw your website somewhere in the search results – maybe at the top, maybe on the bottom, maybe on the 15th page, it doesn't matter, maybe they saw it in a different country or whatever, but they saw it somewhere – and not only that, but they were interested in whatever the little Google summary was, the title and description, and they clicked to get to your site. Those are the search queries that you're seeing here. This is a lot more useful to you than some arbitrary term that you had pulled out of a keyword tool and you're now trying to optimize for. This is an actual result. Google sent you traffic from this particular search and decided that this page on your site was relevant to what the searcher had asked for.

BEN SETTLE: Just so I'm clear on that, instead of using the Google Keyword Tool and all that, you should be looking at the search query in your Google Analytics account.

JIM YAGHI: Yes, because the Google Keyword Tool is about other people's data, whereas the search query reports for your site…

BEN SETTLE: See, this is what I like about this because it's far more tailored to what you're doing. I like how you put that. You're looking at other people's results and not yours. It's kind of like when people say, "That subject line killed it for that guy over there, so I'm going to use it for my list," they're missing the whole point. This reminds me a lot of that kind of thinking.

JIM YAGHI: Totally, because they're always looking at somebody else's result and trying to make it theirs, when the only thing that matters is what's your result? For me, I care how are people finding my site already much more than I do about how can I make people find my site for some crazy-ass term that I think is going to get me shitloads of traffic.

BEN SETTLE: This is a little tangent, but I'm just curious. Do you use this data when you're doing your AdWords campaigns too, for keywords?

JIM YAGHI: I do and I use it for my email writing. I use it for a lot of stuff, yeah.

BEN SETTLE: I'm just thinking, because that would seem to make more sense than using the keyword tool.

JIM YAGHI: I do use the keyword tool for AdWords because, unlike with this, AdWords works off the keywords, whereas organic search works off the actual search query.

BEN SETTLE: Okay, I was just curious. I didn't mean to go on a tangent.

JIM YAGHI: No, it's cool. I think that was a good question.

BEN SETTLE: Once in a while I sound like I know what I'm talking about when it comes to this stuff.

JIM YAGHI: It was an interesting question. It is a point to consider because AdWords tends to not favor the long tail, the exact search, but this SEO does favor the long tail and that's what we're working with here. We're looking for the long tail. Now what we have in front of us is the actual set of search queries that have had our site discovered. Which page is Google sending people to? This is a critical question to ask yourself. Let me just give an example here from my site, just so that I can have a reference point. Unfortunately, this has like 5,000 keywords in one page, so it's being extremely slow. Let me reduce that. Let's do 500. I have like 197,000 ideas here for articles.

BEN SETTLE: You'll never run out of content ideas. That's what I like about it.

JIM YAGHI: Exactly. *Rhianna sex tape* – 135 hits have come to my site for *rhianna sex tape.* Isn't that amazing, considering I'm a marketer? So, let's say *rhianna sex tape* just to keep it interesting. So up at the very top you're going to see that there's a Primary Dimension of Keyword and then there's a menu for Secondary Dimension. If you click that, what you can do now is choose a second dimension to look at, because all you're seeing now is the actual search query, and what we want to know is which page did that search query send people to? We're going to look under that and look at the Secondary Dimension, Landing Page underneath Traffic Sources. Traffic Sources is the category and then Landing Pages. Now the table that you're seeing is going to be updated to show the second column, so you've got the Keyword column and then you have a Landing Page column. That essentially tells you which page specifically at your site people were sent to when they had run that search and clicked your site.

What you've got to understand is that it is possible that Google has sent somebody to your site for the wrong reason – or not the wrong reason, but they sent them to not an exactly well-matched article to what they were looking for. I mean chances are that someone who's looking for *rhianna sex tape* is actually looking for the Rhianna sex tape, right? And yet this is a very popular term on my site, and it's going to an article called "Rhianna Sex Tape, Apple Logo Designer, Too Big to Be Followed."

I'm going to actually open the page, because that's just the URL. You can click the little arrow at the top to see what's on that page. The actual article on my site is called, "Rhianna Sex Tape, Apple Logo Designer, Too Big to Be Followed." When you actually go through it you're going to find that it's an article about – well, it was a news item initially. It talks about how Rhianna and J. Cole denied claims about a sex tape etc, and then it goes into a marketing lesson. The problem with this is that this is not giving people who are looking for *rhianna sex tape* what they want. In fact, as far as I'm concerned, that's a pretty crappy term. Most likely it's bringing me all the wrong people. They're not actually happy with what they're finding on my site, and I may as well not attract those people at all. Let's take a look at a more useful term here. *How does spyfu work* is an actual search that somebody had run. There's over 50 searches and then clickthroughs to my site, so let's see where that goes. It goes to an article called "Spyfu – How Keyword Spy Tools Spy," and it actually is exactly what they're looking for. It describes how Spyfu works, so I can give myself a big pat on the back because I know that I've given people exactly what they want.

Now, why am I concerned with this? If I have a good match between what the person was searching for – and I'm not talking about a keyword match, by the way. Notice that the search query was not necessarily what the title of the article was. The actual search query was *how does spyfu work.* My title is, "Spyfu – How Keyword Spy Tools Spy," so it's not an exact match. There's nothing magical about copying exactly what the search query was and putting in the title of your thing. You don't have to stump your creativity with the idiotic ungrammatical search queries that people run. This was not always the top article here. All I needed to do was see *how does spyfu work.* What's the intent behind that? Somebody wants to learn how to make use of a keyword tool called Spyfu. They want to know how it works, probably to see if they should buy it, if they should make use of it, or if they're already using it they want to know, "How does it gather its data?" so they can kind of verify the validity of it. When I found this keyword come through to my site, at the time it didn't actually go to this article. It was going to some other article where I had just kind of casually mentioned Spyfu in the article. It wasn't about this topic at all. What I did was I went and created a new article when I saw this and I saw that there was a mis-match between what the person was looking for – *how does spyfu work* – and the article they were being sent to, some article about keyword research. It wasn't a complete exact match. If they were to arrive on this page they wouldn't have felt like, "Oh, this is relevant to what I wanted." Google thought it was relevant enough to show, but I know it wasn't relevant to them, so what I did was I created an article that specifically addresses that intent. It tells them how Spyfu works, it shows them how it works, and kind of talks about the advantages and disadvantages of the program, and then it sells something at the end. The result of that is that the next time that Google found somebody searching for *how does spyfu work,* it had a much better related article to show at my site. That's #1.

#2, that next person who got to see this article actually sat there and read through it because it was obvious at face value as soon as they arrived, "This article is going to address whatever I'm looking for." They went through it, they spent some time at the site, they probably connected and engaged with my other content, and they signed up to my newsletter, some of them, and some of them bought products from me. I don't know because I don't track all this stuff, but it's very likely that that has happened. Because of that, Google realized, "Hey, this seems to be a good matching site for this particular search term," and next time someone else does that same search, they're going to be more likely to recommend my site and that specific page to that person, and keep doing it every time that happens. So what I'm doing is building up a variety of different articles that handle all the different intents that people have. Like I said, I have 157,000 search queries all matched up to articles. Ideally you want to cover as many different long tail intents as possible. Ben, do you have some questions or should I just give you some pointers on how to go through your keyword information?

BEN SETTLE: Do what you're going to do and then I thought at the end if you could just summarize the how-to stuff like, "Okay, here's what you do – bam, bam, bam." This stuff makes sense, what you're doing here, because otherwise people will just think, "Oh yeah." They're not going to believe it works unless you explain it like this, because it's not sexy. It's not ninja, right?

JIM YAGHI: No, it's not ninja. That's the problem.

BEN SETTLE: It's good for us. So, it's cool how you're doing it, that's fine.

JIM YAGHI: It's not like, "Take this pill and you're going to drop 100 pounds by tomorrow."

BEN SETTLE: Exactly, and I'll write something in the beginning of the transcript that this is kind of technical, but the how-to's of it are pretty easy. Just read through it so you understand it. It's fine. Do what you've got to do.

JIM YAGHI: The background of how it works is technical, but it's actually very easy. There are a few things to keep in mind if you're going to use this exercise to build a lot of content. You want to be constantly adding content, whatever the keywords are telling you. If they're telling you that there are intents that you need to cover, then by all means cover those, but if you still don't have enough data to be able to do that, just keep writing your articles or your content and keep posting them so that you can have more useful stuff. The whole objective is to have a resource site. That's how you become an authority. You have a resource site on a particular niche topic, and then you have an article for every possible question that anybody in your audience is going to think to ask, any query that they have, any idea that they'd like to know about. You're constantly trying to build up a giant database of all the different things on your site.

When you go through your keywords you're going to find sometimes it says, "not provided" and there's nothing you can do about that, so don't worry about it. You need to move on. If you find your name in there, it's going to be in there. That's not anything to get excited about it. If you find the names of your products in there, again it's nothing to get excited about it. Basically, what this is telling you is you don't have enough content on there.

I've seen people who have these really highly-trafficked sites, they get a lot of JV traffic and blah blah blah, and you look at their analytics and all they have is just these terms that you cannot do anything with. You can't write an article on the basis of these terms because they're just names of the product, they're the name of the author or names of a few people, and they're not useful terms. The reason is because all they have at their site is sales content, squeeze pages, and stuff like that. Yes, you want to have sales pages and follow-up materials, but you need to keep in mind that you're trying to address questions that people are trying to find answers for from your target audience. The kinds of keywords that are useful, though, are things that tell you a specific intent. Here when I scroll through these, the #1 search term on my site is *jim yaghi.* Wonderful, I can't do anything with that. Almost all my site is going to be relevant to that term. Then I've got a bunch of "not provided" that are really high traffic. Then I've got very high traffic for *landing page generator.* The page it's going to is actually very well-related, but the problem with the term is it's so broad that you don't really know what it's about.

Yeah, you probably have one idea about what it might be. They're looking for some kind of a generator program that creates landing pages, but for a lot of people a landing page means something different. What kind of landing page are you talking about? Are you talking about a squeeze type of a landing page? Are you talking about a splash kind of a landing page? Are you looking for a Facebook landing page? Are you looking for a mobile app landing page? It's so broad, I don't know what that term actually means, so if it was me I wouldn't even focus on creating relevant content for a broad keyword like that. What you're looking for is the long tail, meaning multiple-word things, especially questions, so let's keep going. *PPC domination,* that's a product of mine. *Free landing page generator,* again too broad. I'm just going to keep going. *Landing page generator* – these are all the top ones. You're actually going to find your golden nuggets in the very low volume ones, the ones that get 1 and 2 clicks.

BEN SETTLE: That's the most interesting part of this, because that is counter-intuitive.

JIM YAGHI: Yeah, because most people are going to go look at the highest-clicked ones and try to work with that, but that's not what you're trying to do. What you're trying to do is to go wide. You're trying to cast a wide net and get as much of that audience as possible to find your site and find the relevant content on there that's useful to them. By the way, this whole technique, Ben – you know how we were talking the other day about how most of the major innovations and inventions were actually done by people who had no business being in that field in the first place? I actually got the inspiration for this idea – I didn't actually take the technique from anybody. I came up with the technique on my own, but the inspiration for this idea came from book by the name of *The New Rules of Marketing & PR*. I forget the name of the author, but this book was talking about how today people are looking for those niche type of things, and what they use the internet for is to find those little nichey topics, to find that independent artist, for example.

The internet did huge things for them, but not because the independent artist now has a way to market himself, but rather because there are people who are interested in finding the independent artists and they want to listen to their music. They're not looking for the mainstream pop music stuff that you can see in the media. On the internet, you can now do things that you couldn't do before. If you have a very specific need like, "I want to lose weight in time for prom," you can find an article or a video or whatever that will tell you how to lose weight in time for prom. The other day I was looking up videos on how to sleep correctly on your stomach and how to correct sleeping on your stomach. These are not the kinds of things that one used to be able to find before the internet. That's what the internet is allowing us to do, but how do you be that guy who has all of those answers? It's by doing this exercise. It's by looking at what people are searching for, the long tail searches, and giving them what they're looking for in terms of intent. I'm going to actually move down into the much-less-searched keywords here. *How to make your video viral.* That's a very clear intent, right?

BEN SETTLE: Yeah, that could actually be a straight title for an article.

JIM YAGHI: Oh yeah, you can use that as your article title if you want. I actually have several articles on this topic at my site because I uncovered one of these terms bringing me traffic at one point, so I decided, "Okay, let's answer this question." Then I found another question about it, like *why do baby videos go viral.* That was another one. Someone was asking *why do videos with babies in them go viral,* so I did another article on why baby videos go viral, and so on. I built up three or four articles on this topic, and now I get all kinds of traffic about viral content, based on this. The point is that this is a useful search term to me. If I find this in my analytics, I can actually go now and check, "Where is it going? Is it going to the right page? Does this page specifically answer this question?" If not, I'm going to create an article that answers this question specifically.

BEN SETTLE: To kind of keep it on track, because I kind of lost track because of my low attention span, when you find these terms, they don't have to go in the title, right? It's not like you have to force it.

JIM YAGHI: No, you don't have to do anything with that search query except pretend somebody asked you, "How do you make your video go viral?" If you know the answer, write an article that answers it, and that's it. Don't worry about using the specific words, because that's Google's job, to figure out that these things are related.

BEN SETTLE: I find that so liberating because you don't have to worry about these keywords and stuff. You can just write.

JIM YAGHI: Exactly. You don't even have to put it in the title. I had an article pulled out on how to make a video go viral, but you know which one it's actually sending people to for that particular one? It's sending them to *what elements make a video go viral.* For whatever reason, it has determined that this is the best matching article for their intent. I'm not interested in changing Google's mind about this, because either way it's still my content and it's still marketing my stuff.

BEN SETTLE: Yeah, it just makes sense.

JIM YAGHI: So that's all I had on these pointers. Would you like me to give you the summary?

BEN SETTLE: Yeah, if you could just do a how-to summary for the people who just want to skip to the end, because they trust you already and they know you know what you're talking about. They just want to know how to do it. You're talking to them now, like "Here's what you do."

JIM YAGHI: Here's what you do.

Step 1: Make sure you have a Google Analytics account from analytics.google.com.

Step 2: If you use WordPress, you want to install a Google Analytics plugin and associate your account with it.

Step 3: Begin posting your content as normal. You need to do this for at least 14 different days, with an article a day at least, in order to start getting the data that we need in order to do this exercise.

Step 4: Keep adding content ongoingly, regardless of what's going on with your analytics and the SEO. Just make sure that you keep adding content to your site and that it's being updated regularly.

BEN SETTLE: If you're writing an email a day, like I recommend, you're already doing this.

JIM YAGHI: Exactly.

Step 5: Now look at your analytics account every day. The section to go to is under Traffic Sources > Sources > Search > Organic. That will get you to a section of your Analytics account that tells you which search queries have brought you traffic in the past to one or more of your articles that you have.

Step 6: Make sure you set your date range to as long as the website has existed, so you can see the full range of data.

Step 7: You're going to add the Secondary Dimension of Landing Page from the Secondary Dimension menu. It should be under Traffic Sources > Landing Pages. So it'll be in the main section of the site. Your Primary Dimension is Keyword. Secondary Dimension is Landing Page. This will add a second column to your data so you can see which search query brought the visitor, and which page they landed on when they arrived at your site.

Step 8: You're going to try to create a better match between the searcher's intent – between the search query they had run – and the landing page that they arrived at. What you're checking is, "Is this a good match for what they had wanted – the intent behind the search that they'd made?" If yes, leave it and move on to another one, or just add more content from your own head. You don't have to worry about this keyword stuff if you don't have enough keywords to be able to do that. Wait for more information.

If, on the other hand, you find that there is a search query that is interesting to you, it's a good search query as far as you're concerned and you'd like to be able to attract that person to your content, or people like that to your content, then the next time around you're going to need a better article to bring them in. So you're going to create a new article based on that keyword.

If they're asking a question, and the article that they're going to does not answer that question, write an article that answers that question, and you're done.

Step 9: Repeat.

BEN SETTLE: That sounds good. That's it. That's the whole thing. Just to clarify the one point, in writing these articles you don't even have to write a Q&A article necessarily, but you are answering that question in that article. It doesn't have to be like someone asked it to you via email, just so people are clear on that.

JIM YAGHI: You don't have to pose it as a question in the title. You don't have to use the exact wording that they had used. This technique does not have any technical bits and pieces. The only thing that is technical is looking at the site statistics. How do people arrive at your site? Did they get what they wanted? If not, create an article that gives people like that what they want the next time they see your site.

BEN SETTLE: Nice, man. Dude, that's pretty cool. Any final thoughts? I'm going to insist that you give your URL so people can find more of your brilliance.

JIM YAGHI: www.JimYaghi.com/subscribe. That's where you can get on my mailing list where you can learn more about the technique and a bunch of other inventions. Actually, I came up with some of these inventions with Ben.

BEN SETTLE: I'm a good guinea pig and I have all the bloody holes in my arms and stuff from all the testing you've done.

JIM YAGHI: All the experimentation that's been done on you. [laughing]

BEN SETTLE: That's why I walk funny. That's why one of my eyes blinks for no reason sometimes, and I have twitches and nervous tics.

Chapter 8
How to Build an Audience of Hot, *Eager-to-Buy* Customers from Scratch and Without Spending any Money

BEN SETTLE: I'm coming at this from a fanboy kind of position. Like I'm all into having a bigger list and I'm all into having a bigger influence, but you don't really talk about building a list. You talk about building an audience, is that a completely different animal?

DANNY INY: It's not completely different, but it's like a square and a rectangle kind of thing. An audience is sort of a kind of a list. The reason why I make that distinction is in a perfect world if everyone is doing exactly what they should be doing, your list is your audience. In the real world, a lot of people build lists in stupid ways and send them stupid things, and generally speaking they see a list as a way of aggregating the contact information of random people who might eventually buy something from you if you send them enough offers. They don't create a situation where people actually engage with you as a person, with you as a business. There isn't a relationship there. There isn't a dynamic, which means it's not a warm list, it's a cold list. If you want to go really hardcore marketing-speak you can see building an audience as building a business that's driven by a super-warm hot list. They trust you. They like you. They are following you and listening to you because you help them, but also because they feel a connection with you and you stand for something that matters to them. We talk about a list and we talk about email because having this massive audience of people that is really engaged with you only does you so much good as a business if you have no kind of easy-to-access and reliable way of communicating with them. So, you're going to want to have them on an email list, but the fact that they're on your email list is almost kind of a secondary symptom of the fact that they're a part of your audience and they're engaged with you.

Something that is kind of very different in terms of the cart and the horse kind of order is that for most internet marketers, for example, for most businesses in general, the people who know them are for the most part on their list, and a lot of the people who are on their list may not even know them all that well. They stumbled onto a website, they registered to download something, and they only vaguely remember you, like "Who is this guy that's sending me stuff?" If you're really building an audience – and this is something that we really experience – a lot more people know who we are than are on our list, and people think we're a lot bigger than we are.

BEN SETTLE: Which adds to your positioning and credibility.

DANNY INY: Exactly. I'm trying to think of what's a good comparable example. Not delusions of grandeur, I'm not Tony Robbins, but you may not be subscribed to Tony Robbins' newsletter or email list, and you may not have bought any of his books, but you still know who he is. You know roughly what he stands for and you may feel an affinity for that, even if you haven't really consumed a lot of his stuff because he's been featured in enough places in enough ways, and he stands for something. He figures into the conversation of at least the target audience that he wants to matter to.

BEN SETTLE: I want to back up just a little bit here. Tell me the story about how you fell into this mindset of building an audience. While everybody else is out there just talking about list building, you're talking about audience. Were you always into this or is this kind of an epiphany you had, or what's the story behind that?

DANNY INY: It really kind of crystallized for me over a whole bunch of time. I started doing what I'm doing right now in 2010. I've been a marketing strategy consultant for a while. I built this training program that teaches people how to really understand and how to do that well, and I did exactly what I teach all my students not to do. I built this massive training program before I had an audience, which is a huge mistake. Do as I say, not as I do. I've made these mistakes so you don't have to, kind of thing. But I built this thing and I'm like, "Okay, I need to reach people. I need to tell them about it," so I started blogging. I only vaguely had a sense of how blogging works and why it should work, but I kind of accepted it on faith that you blog and somehow customers come. I did that, as lot of people do. The challenge there is that if you're just accepting it on faith because someone's told you that that's the case, if you don't see how the dots connect it's probably because you're missing something important, so the dots aren't going to connect. That's what I experienced. I worked really hard, I wrote a lot of stuff, and nothing really happened. It was only as I started to write things and kind of stumbled onto, "What are the things that really matter to people, that people really connect with?" and putting it in places that they are.

I did a lot of guest posting, especially as I was getting started. You create content, you put it in front of people, and people respond. You start realizing, "Hey, this isn't just about some faceless nameless thing where you run these ads or do this loophole trick and somehow something starts to happen. These are real people who are reading real things that you're producing and really engaging with it and connecting." Very intuitively, you do more of the things that people are connecting with and people are appreciating.

And this is kind of the biggest irony. It started to become really clear to me that a lot of people were wondering about this topic of audience and this topic of engagement. What is engagement? How do you build engagement? There was this really big gap in the market, at least at the time – this was 2011 – in that almost everything that everyone was writing about engagement was about how to engage your audience. It sort of pre-supposed that you've got this big audience. "If you're Coca-Cola and you've got 400 bazillion people who know who you are, here's how you make them more engaged," stuff like that. What if you're just getting started? What if your email list has got 3 subscribers – you, your other email address, and your cat? What do you do then? How do you build an engaged audience if you're starting from scratch? I started to see that question asked again and again and again in different permutations. By this time, I had started to build a little bit of an audience, a few hundred people on my list, a few thousand people who knew who I was – hardly a global phenomenon, but something – and I wanted to start answering that question, but I looked around and I started asking other people, "How did you do it?" and their answers were all different – different from me and different from each other, and yet they'd all been successful, so clearly this stuff worked.

I realized I couldn't answer this question well. I was just setting out originally to create a piece of content answering the question people were asking, but as I gathered more information this morphed into my book, *Engagement from Scratch,* which is about how to build an engaged audience from scratch, from zero, and features the input of 30 different people who've done it in different ways to different scales. In aggregating all this information and getting everyone's perspective, and then once the book was published doing a ton of interviews and answering a ton of questions, I kind of fell into this expertise, but it really just started as me trying to answer a question that I saw a bunch of people asking. It wasn't until I got really deep into trying to answer that question that I realized how powerful and important it was, and it really shaped and changed the way I look at what it takes to build a successful thriving business.

BEN SETTLE: Let's talk about that real quick. When you started coming to these realizations and applying them to what you were doing, what was the result? Was it like night and day results? I imagine over time you probably increased your bottom line quite a bit, or how did that work? Was it fast or did it take time?

DANNY INY: Night and day results in a bunch of different ways. We've been pretty transparent about what our numbers have been at Firepole Marketing. We've published about it in a bunch of different places. 2011 was the first real year of operation for us, just building a foundation. We started January 1, 2011 at zero, no traffic, no subscribers, nothing. And in that year, 2011, even though we worked really hard, we were just getting the word out, building the foundations, and we made maybe a couple tens of thousands of dollars, maybe not. I don't even remember where the money came from, but most of the money that I made that year came from my offline consulting business. In 2012, building on that foundation, at this point all of my income came from Firepole Marketing. We grossed over a quarter of a million dollars, and this year (we're recording this at the end of 2013) we almost tripled that again. We're doing somewhere around $700,000 this year. Now is that fast? Yes and no. Yes, it's fast. By most objective measures it's fast, but the first year you've really got to build those foundations and build those connections and build that good will. In that sense it feels slow, and especially in an online world that's full of promises of overnight riches where people's expectations of what is a reasonable scale and timeframe for a return on investments, it doesn't feel fast.

BEN SETTLE: That's a pretty big jump. You go from one extreme to the next. You say it took like a year, and everybody probably looks at you and says, "Oh yeah, that happened fast," but they didn't see all that work you put into it. What were some of the things you did to lay that foundation that you talked about, that year where you were building everything up?

DANNY INY: There's a very specific set of strategies that we teach, and they all group into three categories. There's participating in communities, there's contributing to communities, and there's leading communities, and they build one on top of the other.

The first step in terms of tactically, tangibly, what did we actually do, it's contributing to communities. The people that you want to reach, they're already out there online. They're already aggregating in communities that are led by other people. So you go and you don't try to grab the bull horn, but you start contributing. In the world of blogging that looks like leaving a lot of comments on blog posts – not stupid "Great post" type comments, but real stuff. It's got to have been a post that you actually thought was good or that actually raised a question, and really participate in the conversation. Yeah, you get a link. People see you and they can click on your name and go back and check out your site, but you're not doing it primarily for that. You're doing it because you want to start getting recognized in the conversation. You want the owners of those blogs to recognize you as someone who has something to say and something to contribute. We use benchmarks of subscriber numbers, but it's not about the subscribers numbers. I'll tell someone, "You can probably get your first 100-200 subscribers by leaving comments on blog posts that way," and it doesn't have to be blog posts. You can be participating in forums, it can be a lot of different things, but you're participating in somebody else's community. The idea is not to get those let's say 200 subscribers before moving on. The idea is that if you get 200 subscribers in this way, by the time you move on enough people will know you or have a sense of who you are that you can do the next thing in an effective way.

The next thing is to contribute to somebody else's community. At this point they know who you are. They trust you a little bit. They're willing to accept your contribution. In the blogging world that means guest posting. They'll let you write a blog post that you'll publish on their site to their audience, and a lot more people are going to read it and see it because people read that blog and they don't read yours yet. You're still going to have to work. I hear stories from people, and some of them are friends – John Marlow is a friend of mine, Peter Sandini is a friend of mine – and they talk about getting hundreds and hundreds of subscribers from a single guest post. Yes, that can happen. I've done that. It's happened on occasion, but often you might publish a guest post and not get tons and tons of subscribers. You'll get some subscribers. You're still going to have to hustle. You're going to have to put in the time and do the work and do a whole bunch of writing. But in doing that, you grow your audience, you grow your subscriber base. You can get to maybe 1,000 subscribers by publishing this day. But more importantly, a lot more people are going to read your stuff and get to know who you are than just the ones who come and subscribe and check you out and join your active audience base.

BEN SETTLE: Just from a practical point of view, the guys and gals reading this are hardcore emailers. I don't do a lot of what you're saying, not because I don't agree with it. I'm just not that internet social. I just don't make myself that available, and my strategy is completely different than yours. I'm behind what you're saying. I think it's really cool, but when I do participate, which is once in a while, I find that when you answer somebody's question or something – like you're saying, participating – whatever you write to someone, there's an email for you to send to your list. You've just written something that can go out almost as-is to your email list. So, it's not like you're just doing this and it's all this work and you have to wait for it to pay off. You can use that answer to write an article, to write another email, a blog post or whatever. I'm just saying that primarily for the people who are reading this because they might be thinking, "Oh man, I've got to do all this work?" But really if they're going to do the work anyway, why not get this extra benefit out of building an audience, you know?

DANNY INY: Absolutely, it's a really good point and it's an important insight to add to this. None of this is lost. It's all really useful, and it allows you to kind of pilot test your messaging. You leave a comment on a blog post, and if nobody cares, nobody cares. But let's say you're not participating on a blog that has three readers, because what's the point? You're participating in active communities, so a lot of people are going to read these comments, and people will respond. Maybe they'll appreciate it. Maybe they'll have a response to what you're saying. Maybe it's going to be controversial, and this is going to give you a sense of what is and what's not going to resonate. That's the other side of what's so important about doing this kind of in this order. I don't leave comments on blog posts. I don't participate in that way anymore because it's not a good use of my time, so it's not something that I do forever. It's just something you do in that kind of early stage of people getting to know you. But you're not going to be well-positioned to go and write a blog post that people are going to respond well to before you've participated a little bit in the conversation and seen what people are engaging with.

BEN SETTLE: This is really good for someone who wants to get into a new market.

DANNY INY: That's also a really important insight. This assumes you're starting from scratch. If you already have relationships with your market, if you already have some authority, you can potentially skip some of these steps. This really assumes you're starting absolutely from zero. Nobody knows who you are. You're just getting to know the market and the online world, so it works from zero. You can skip ahead if you've already got a list, you've got an audience, you've got relationships with other players and so forth.

BEN SETTLE: I like that. I was using myself as an example. The reason I don't do it is because I don't need to. But if I was starting from scratch in another market I would totally do that. That's a great way to do it. I've observed people do it, but I never really thought of doing it myself. I'm interested in certain topics that have nothing to do with business or anything to do with anything I sell, and I've noticed exactly what you're saying. There are certain people who kind of constantly just contribute, and sooner or later everybody's like, "Hey, when are you going to get a blog going?"

because they're building that reputation.

DANNY INY: Exactly. The rule of thumb that I teach students is that the tactics and strategies that you're employing should grow the total size of your audience – and you can use your list subscriber base as a heuristic for that – by 10-25% per month. If it's less than 10% then it's time for you to scale up to something that is getting you better traction. Assuming you've done it in this kind of step-by-step way, if your audience has grown to the point that you can't grow it by 10-25% in a month by, for example, leaving all these comments, move on to guest posting. But don't try to aim too much higher than 25% per month because you're kind of boxing out of your weight class. I curate an audience, I lead an audience, and the reason why I have this engaged audience is that I've been very careful about what I put in front of them. They've learned to trust me, so I'm very protective of that audience. If you're trying to grow more than 10-25% per month – with exceptions, but again as a rule of thumb – then you're probably asking me to take more of a chance on you with the relationships I've built with my audience than you've earned. It'll work sometimes, but sometimes you'll kind of burn your bridges, and that's a tricky thing to do.

BEN SETTLE: That makes sense. I didn't mean to derail you on all that stuff. Were you building toward the third step?

DANNY INY: Yeah, the third step is leading an audience, kind of having the person who owns the audience, who leads the audience, handing you their microphone. It's kind of like guest posts are a really tiny version of that. They might do a teleseminar or a webinar or a podcast interview or some kind of co-promotion where they're endorsing you. With a guest post it's kind of an implied endorsement. It's like, "Obviously I wouldn't run this on my site if I didn't think it was this good, but this is this person's post." Here they're saying, "Danny is doing this webinar event. Danny is putting on this online workshop. I think you should attend." They're explicitly endorsing you. They're explicitly putting out that message, and that's when the speed of growth really accelerates a lot faster. You don't have to have commented on somebody's blog and guest posted on their blog before getting to that, but you have to have commented on enough blogs for people to know who you are to be able to have earned those first few guest posts, and those guest posts earn you more across the market that you're in. Once you've done enough of those, you've created enough value for these audiences for some of the owners of those audiences to take a chance and endorse you in that way. Then if that's gone well, that's enough for others who lead audiences in this space to do the same.

BEN SETTLE: You look at it now and say, "Oh, that's simple," but really, man, I don't know too many people doing this kind of thing. I don't know anybody who's actually done this in the exact way you're talking about. If they did it was an accident. They didn't do it methodically.

DANNY INY: Well, that's the thing. Hindsight is 20/20. This is exactly what I did, and it's not because I'm such a genius. It's because I tried a lot of things and I paid attention. What I'm teaching and sharing is the stuff that worked, and all the rest is not relevant.

BEN SETTLE: I get it. And you've been helping a lot of people since then do this very thing, right? This is what you do now, or one of the things you do.

DANNY INY: This is what we do. It's something that we've come to really care about and evangelize. We teach the specifics of the commenting and the guest posting and the webinars and all the specific tactics and logistics, but we teach it because it's the best way for people to learn this more generalized process of getting in front of a group of people who care about the stuff that you care about, and leading them in a way that they want and need to be led.

BEN SETTLE: Let's talk about how you help people. Tell us about this thing you're doing and how it's going to help them, anyone who wants to build an audience.

DANNY INY: What we're putting on is an online workshop that is titled "Bridging Your Passion, Purpose, and Prosperity in 2014," so there's a few things there. There's a lot of myths out there. People talk about "All you need is passion. Follow your passion and the money will come," and it's not that simple. You have to find your passion. You have to bridge it with a purpose, and you have to follow a process that leads to prosperity.

This workshop is going to teach you how to do that – how to take the things that you care about and merge them with a plan that can lead to real prosperity in the way that I kind of touched on a little bit in this interview – and do something that gets you there this year in 2014. That's basically what we're talking about.

People are going to learn a lot there. It's completely free no-strings training, but all that leads into our Business Audience Master Class, the 14-week training program that teaches you step-by-step detail-by-detail how to do everything that I've just described.

It's not just "Here you go, a bunch of information, now you're on your own, best of luck." In terms of my identity, in terms of my purpose, my passion, it's education and it's business. We don't sell information. We're an education company and we're teachers who will teach you how to do this. We will hold you by the hand and answer your questions and guide you and get you to where you want to go.

We have students that we exchange pages of emails with every week, answering their questions and advising them on their strategy, and we're happy to do it. As my student, your success is my success, and I take that very seriously.

It's a plan that you can follow to get from wherever you are to where you want to go – true prosperity, leading an audience that cares about the things you care about, and making things better for them. There's a mission, there's purpose, but there's prosperity. You're making money doing it. It's incredibly lucrative and incredibly rewarding, but it's not just the plan, it's all the support and guidance that you need to get there.

BEN SETTLE: You know what I like about this thing you're doing is – at least the way you've been explaining it here – if someone gets on my list and they find me through a search engine or whatever, it might take a week or two or three for them to warm up to me, but this way they come to you already warmed up. I mean I get people like that, don't get me wrong, but not the majority. I'm guessing most people reading this transcript don't get hot people coming in like they would the way you're describing. It seems like it could or should shorten the time span between when someone becomes a lead and when they become a buyer.

DANNY INY: That's the really cool thing about this. All this sounds really warm and fuzzy and make people really happy and engage with them, and all that's true and I believe that, but it also has very solid, very tangible business outcomes that it creates.

One of the things I really believe is people have this kind of mistaken dichotomy in their head around, "You've always got to choose between doing the good thing and the right thing on the one hand, or kind of the smart business thing on the other hand," and I don't think that's accurate. I think in most cases the right thing and the smart thing are the same thing. We've been able to do this. We've created all this amazing value for our audience. We've made so many people so happy. We've also made a lot of money by doing it, and that's the beauty of it.

I heard this stat somewhere, and obviously this will vary enormously by industry to industry, business to business, but if you ask an old-school internet marketer how much money should you expect to make from your list, a number that I've heard is $1 per subscriber per month kind of as an average target. By building an audience in this way and having people truly engage and connect, we've seen we can do anywhere between $3-$8 per subscriber per month, depending on the month. That's a lot of money. That's a big difference.

BEN SETTLE: That is a big difference. I always get a kick out of it when people come up with those numbers - $1 per subscriber – because I'm like you, man. I'm doing way better than that, and it's because I've probably been implementing some of the stuff that you teach without even realizing it. It's got to be that engagement, so I'm excited about this, man. It's something I wish I had known when I was starting. I took like 10 years to figure this stuff out.

DANNY INY: You and me both.

BEN SETTLE: I don't think people understand the frustration levels that you go through. I've heard your story how you went from $10,000 here, $10,000 there, to all the sudden $700,000 in a year. That's not a fluke. That's not luck. That's a methodical way of doing things. I'm going to assume that you have a lot of students who've done just as well, if not better.

DANNY INY: We've got many, many hundreds of students. I think we worked with about 800 students this year.

BEN SETTLE: Can you tell us maybe a story about some dramatic examples of someone who came with no knowledge and they were frustrated, and then suddenly they were doing really good? Are there any stories like that that you have?

DANNY INY: Sure, we've got tons of them. We don't share specifics about our students because we respect their privacy, so I'll share some specifics and I'll share some of the general examples, which is kind of what I actually care about the most.

As a specific example, I've got a guy who was thinking about starting a blog forever, and playing around with it and never really got – never mind traction, never even really got a blog up and running. Through this program he got his blog up and running. He's been guest posting and been featured on a ton of major blogs. I could say mine but it sounds like, well, he's my student, but we're actually really strict about who we let publish, but he's been featured on a ton of other major blogs as well.

His list is growing very fast and it's important to say this – it's not just that his list is growing. I mean you can buy leads and it's not that big a deal, but they're all super-engaged, super-warm, and he's turning it into a real business doing exactly what he wants to do.

There's the example of a student of mine. Again, I won't share his name, but I'll share some specifics because he's published them in various places on the internet so they're public. A young guy, he's 21 years old or something, a student at Yale University, and he told me, "Your course is the best course I've done this semester." He followed this process and he's building and leading a community. He's teamed up with – do you know who Susan Cain is?

BEN SETTLE: I'm not familiar, but I'm very unfamiliar with most people.

DANNY INY: She wrote a book about introverts. She's got a TED talk that's been viewed like a bazillion times, so she's like his idol in the space. She's kind of the expert authority in his space, and he's teamed up with her and they're doing all these really cool things together, and it's by following these steps.

We've got a ton of examples like this. People have launched communities in all kinds of different areas, people who are making really good money. They've replaced their income, they've quit their jobs. I'm very against those "Sign up for this program and quit your job in 3 days." It's not like that. People work hard, but if you work hard and put in the time you'll get there. I won't say fast, but I'll say a lot faster than you would by doing any other nonsense.

I said I'd share some specifics and I'd also share a general example. The general example that I see, and this is what I get really excited about, is that as you go into our forums and you go into our alumni groups where students interact, and you just look at the questions and answers from people who are brand new and compare it with people who've been with us for a few months, there's a level of savviness, a level of sophistication that is just really impressive and exciting to me.

It's something that they're taking and applying to build something real online, but something that ports really well to all kinds of different things that they might want to do. That's not why anyone signs up. Nobody signs up because they want the general education ability to do whatever in whatever context, but for me as a teacher that has me excited.

BEN SETTLE: Thanks for doing this early. I appreciate it.

For more information about what Danny Iny is teaching, go here:

www.EmailPlayers.com/audience

(**NOTE:** This offer comes and goes,
the above link may be dead
depending on when you read this)

Chapter 9
"Dirt Cheap" Ways
to Use Your Local Post Office
to Pack Your Email List
with the Best,
Most Eager-to-Buy Customers
You Can Possibly Find

BEN SETTLE: Craig, tell us about your business and maybe some of the clients you've helped with direct mail – I know you and I worked with Carbon Copy Pro together there briefly – and maybe some of the successes you've seen and had with direct mail.

CRAIG SIMPSON: Okay. Right now, one of my biggest clients is Beach Body. You've probably heard of them. They're the big fitness company. They sell P90X and 10-Minute Trainer and all those. I've done some mailings for their 10-Minute Trainer product, but the biggest product I'm marketing for them right now is they have a beauty line called Derm Exclusive. It's basically an anti-wrinkle cream. We're sending out hundreds of thousands, and maybe soon to be millions of sales pieces promoting this Derm Exclusive face glop.

I also work with a chain of pet food stores called Pet Supplies Plus. The large chain is 250. I'm working with their top 20 stores doing mailings for them. The interesting thing between say a Beach Body Derm Exclusive product and a pet food store, you'd look at them from the outside and you'd think, "Wow, these guys don't really have anything in common. One's selling pet food and one's selling face cream. What are the similarities?" The interesting thing is at the pet food store their avatar client is women who are older and who are affluent, the same category that Beach Body is.

The cool thing is I'm able to take a mail piece that's similar in style and design that sells face cream, and use it to attract the same type of woman to get them into a pet food store, because their characteristics are the same so we're really able to pull two niches and kind of use a similar style for both of them because of who we're going to. Those are the kinds of things that people don't normally consider or think about with direct mail.

So Derm Exclusive is a big client, Pet Supplies Plus is a big client, and then I also work with a lot of smaller medical facilities or dentists or attorneys. I work with a ton of information marketers, a lot in the real estate market, those who are selling "get rich in real estate" types of products. There's probably somebody in just about every niche that I'm working with. Does that kind of give you an overview of some of the people I'm working with and some of the things that I do?

BEN SETTLE: Oh yeah, definitely. Why are people so resistant to using direct mail do you think, especially the internet guys?

CRAIG SIMPSON: That's a great question. I love Doberman Dan because he's so pro-direct mail, and it ties to Gary Halbert. He's got a great story. Online I think the biggest hurdle for them to get over is the cost, because there is a high cost per acquisition to get into the mail. It costs a lot to acquire customers. You can't just run a simple test like you can online.

Online you can spend $100 or $200 or $1,000 and instantly test something out and have results within a few hours. With direct mail, it costs more and it also takes longer. It's a longer process. You don't send a mailing out today and have all your results in tomorrow, but there's a huge difference between a direct mail buyer and an online buyer.

One of my clients was a big publisher in the real estate niche and they did heavy infomercials. I think I mailed over 10 million pieces a year for them, and they also did a lot online. I did an analysis where I took 50,000 buyers who had purchased their product for $151.50 who bought online. I took a different group but the exact same type of buyer from those who bought on TV. They originated from a TV commercial and they spent $151.50 for the same product. Then I took 50,000 direct mail buyers who spent $151.50 from direct mail. So, in this sample size I took 150,000 buyers within the last 16 months and did an analysis to see where their customer values were.

The TV guys had spent twice as much money as the guys who were generated online, and the guys who were from direct mail had spent a third more than those who'd bought off the TV and three times as much as those who had bought online.

So yes, the cost per acquisition was higher, and yes, it took longer to get them in the door, but the return on investment was much greater because they would spend more in the long run. They would stick around longer and we could get them to buy more products and services. So, what I say to somebody who's struggling with, "Hey, online advertising is easy and cheap," I say, "Look at the quality of buyers."

I recently had a conversation with a very well-known online marketer. I'm not going to tell you their name, but they generated close to half million new buyers within the first six months of this year. If I told you who it was you would know who it is. I could tell you offline, but not on this recording here. They were struggling because they could only get $7-12 out of their buyers. So yes, they had sold 500,000 people, but they were only getting $7-12 out of them.

It's a famous online marketer and he's like, "What do I do? How can I get these guys to spend more money?" The answer is direct mail. He's got to find a new avenue to get them in the door so he can create higher-end buyers. I think you'll find it's very common that guys who are just generating online leads are going to have low customer values and are going to have a hard time getting people to buy other products and services and stick with them for the long run.

BEN SETTLE: Have you found this to be the case – I remember Gary Halbert would talk about this – for guys that are just totally online, that if we just added direct mail it's almost like adding another zero to our profits. Is that usually the case from what you've seen?

CRAIG SIMPSON: I would totally agree with that. And why don't more people do it? Well, there's more of a science to it. You have to really think it through when you're spending money on printing and postage. You can't just throw out a simple sales letter. You've got to actually put some thought into it and make sure that it's set up right. You've got a bigger investment so there's bigger risk, but there's also much bigger gain.

BEN SETTLE: And I would imagine way less competition amongst people who are just on the internet.

CRAIG SIMPSON: Right. That's one of the things. When people hear that the postage rates go up they're like, "Oh man, that's no good. It costs more to be in mail." I look at the opposite of it. It doesn't bother me as much when it goes up because you know what it means? Less people are in the mailbox, less saturation, and higher response rates.

BEN SETTLE: I agree with that totally, man. There was this scare that the government would start charging for email. I hope they do, for that very same reason, to get rid of all the competition.

CRAIG SIMPSON: Wouldn't that be interesting? It would only be the savvy marketers that would be left, the guys that are really good, and the email boxes wouldn't be as full. Wouldn't that be interesting if they taxed it or charged you for it?

BEN SETTLE: Everybody would probably on to Facebook, which is free, and the rest of us would make out like bandits. What are some good ways to build an email list through direct mail?

CRAIG SIMPSON: I've found that the best way is to drive people online using direct mail, using an over-sized postcard or what I call a 4-page self-mailer. I send out almost 300 mailings a year and about 100 of those are doing exactly that. They're driving people online. They're building their herd. They're getting email addresses and they're getting people from offline and moving them online, so about a third of the mailings I do every year are focused on that.

I've found you could use a 12-page sales letter to accomplish that, but it's really overkill. What I've found to be the most cost-effective is using an over-sized postcard, say 6" x 11" or 8-1/2" x 5-1/2", using that format or using the format of what I call a 4-page self-mailer, which is basically a sheet of 11x17 paper folded in half, and that gives you four pages of 8-1/2" x 11". Then fold it in half again and it mails at 8-1/2" x 5-1/2". Those two formats work best.

Now, what do we do? We're offering some kind of free report or more information if they go online. For example, if you're selling say a joint pain supplement and you want to build your herd, you're not going to sell the joint pain supplement in the postcard or the 4-page self-mailer. What you're going to do is you're going to sell them about all the great benefits and things that you'll get by going online to learn more about this revolutionary whatever it is, whatever the product is.

A lot of people get confused and think, "I need to sell the product through the postcard or through the self-mailer," when in reality the whole purpose of that is to sell them to go online, because when they go online, that's when you capture their name and email address. So, what we do with direct mail is we drive them online. We get them to opt in, just asking for first and last name and email address. Then we can drive them to wherever we want after that – the video sales letter, the long form online sales letter, whatever it is.

I'm finding that on average we're getting about a 3-5% opt in rate, then conversion on the back end all depends on the pricing. Let's say you get a 5% optin and you're selling a $100 product once they get online. We're getting about 5% of those people to buy. In some cases, the guys that are really good and have the really long sales letters, we're able to get 12-13% conversion rate on that, but the average is 5% optin, 5% conversion. If you're selling a product that's $1000 or more, the conversion rate is closer to 1-2%.

Some tips are to use a self-mailer, keep it simple, and make the copy completely focused on getting them online. Don't try to sell two things. Don't try to sell them on getting online and selling a product. Just sell them on getting online. Then once they're online you can focus on selling your product.

The last thing is make sure you make it completely clear what you want them to do and where you want them to go. If I'm doing a postcard I'm not going to put the URL on there just one time. I know it's a short piece but I'm still going to put the URL on there three or four times. I want to make it so apparent where they're supposed to go that they can't miss it.

Those are a few tips for getting people and building herds with direct mail.

BEN SETTLE: Maybe this is different for everything, but the page that you send people to from the postcard or the self-mailer, is it usually a pretty simple squeeze page or is it an elaborate one? Is it like they've already been sold on putting their name and email in, or should they reiterate everything on that squeeze page?

CRAIG SIMPSON: We've had the most success with a very simple, very plain optin page. We don't put a whole bunch of information on there. It's basically, "Hey, enter your name and email address here and get access to your free report" or whatever it is that we've promoted in the postcard. It's extremely simple and extremely plain.

BEN SETTLE: Great. I guess the next question I have for you has always had me a little concerned because if you ask 10 people you get 10 different answers. You're the master at this so I'm going to ask you, and that's about list brokers. What are some tips on picking a good list broker, because some of them are good and some aren't so good. Do you look for referrals or what's a good way to do that?

CRAIG SIMPSON: First of all, if you don't mind, let me talk about what a list broker does and how they charge, because I think that's helpful. I think a lot of people think, "Man, if I go use a list broker it's going to cost me a bunch of money," but the reality is a list broker is a lot like a real estate broker.

If you go into say your town of Roseburg, Oregon and you want to buy a house, you can go to any real estate broker in Roseburg and they'll show you all the houses on the market. Then if you choose to purchase a house they'll orchestrate the sale of that home, and then they get paid by the person selling the house. The reality is, you don't have to pay for their services. It's the seller who's paying for their services.

In the list business, it's the same. You can go to any list broker and they have access to all the lists that are on the market, and there are over 100,000 of them. They can go get any list on the market and they can show you and give you some recommendations on lists that you should or could rent. If you choose to rent that list they can orchestrate the rental of it, and then they get paid a commission from the list owner. It's not a commission from you.

Let's say you have them do all this research and you didn't find a list you liked, so you don't owe them any money. You don't have to pay them for any of their services. They only collect a commission if you rent a list, and that commission is collected from the list owner, so the great thing about a list broker is it's free.

On how to find them, I have list brokers that I recommend using, but if you're in a major city there's a good chance there's a list broker in your town if it's a major city like New York, Chicago, Los Angeles, San Francisco, those types of places. If you wanted to you could go sit down in their office and interview them like you would any vendor to find out if they're somebody you'd enjoy working with. If not, you can do a search online and there's tons of them to choose from.

All of us work with different types of vendors and we have a feeling of how we'd like to work with them, so you just have to talk to them on the phone and get a good gut feel of whether or not they're somebody you'd feel comfortable working with.

One thing you can look out for is when you're going to them and saying, "Hey, here's my avatar client. Can you go find me a list that looks just like them?" if they come back to you and they recommend just lists that they manage, then their only interest is trying to get you to take their own personal lists. Now, if they come back and they give you lists that not only they manage, but lists that are outside of their management, then they're more likely to look out for your best interests.

When I say manage I mean like a real estate broker if they're the listing agent and they're the ones that are in charge of showing that home. If you went to a real estate broker and they only showed you the homes that they're listing and no one else's listings, then they'd be doing you a disservice. It's the same in the list business. They need to show you other lists outside of the ones that they manage, and if they're not, they're probably not a broker you want to work with. Did that help some?

BEN SETTLE: It definitely does. What about this idea of looking for lists with recency, frequency, and unit of sale? Is that important for us to have in mind as far as picking a specific list?

CRAIG SIMPSON: The RFM – Recency, Frequency, Monetary value – really comes into play when you're dealing with your house file, your internal database of customers and prospects – mainly customers. That's really who it works on.

Let's say you had a big customer base of 50,000 people and you wanted to test a new product or service to them. You could run a RFM score on that list and it could narrow it down to your best customers and you could test it with just them. With renting lists you're not able to do an RFM on them because it's not your data, it's somebody else's. They own it, so you would want to rent a list based off of other sets of criteria rather than the RFM score.

When it comes to renting lists, I'll give you a couple pointers of things that I look for. One of the first things I look for is I want to go to buyers' lists whenever possible. It's not always possible, but whenever possible I want to go after people who have previously purchased something, and previously purchased something through the mail, so they're direct mail buyers.

If you're selling golf clubs, I would like to find a list of those who have bought golf clubs through the mail, or if you're selling golf videos, other people who have bought golf videos through the mail. I want to go to lists that look just like what you're selling. So #1 is buyers.

#2 would be to make sure they're direct mail-responsive, meaning they responded to a prior direct mail campaign.

Then #3 would be recency. I want to make sure that they recently purchased. I don't want to get people that are two or three years old. I want people that purchased in the last 90 days, because they're most likely to buy again.

Those are some of the key things that I look for in picking a list.

BEN SETTLE: Is it a good idea to get your offer working online first where it's cheap to test everything, and then take it offline, or do you think it's better to start offline and then take what you learn from there and go online, like if someone's just starting out.

CRAIG SIMPSON: That's a big question. That's a tough one. It really is dependent on the company, the niche, and what it is you're trying to do. I really don't have an easy answer for that. There are some niches where it makes sense to start out with direct mail, and there are other niches where it doesn't. I work with a lot of financial newsletter guys selling advisory newsletters, and I would much rather test it through direct mail than I would online first, because we know the funnel. We know how well it works. We know exactly the steps to take.

I guess where it changes is if you're saying, "Hey look, I want to build my herd online and I want to use direct mail to drive them to an online funnel." At that point if you're driving them online, that online funnel that you have has to be tested out before you can drive direct mail to it, so in that case you'd want to test it out first.

Let's say you're driving to an online funnel using direct mail and it doesn't work. You don't know at that point is it the direct mail piece? Is it the list? Is it the offer? Is it the funnel? Why didn't it work? Whereas if we can drive to an online funnel that's already proven, and if for some reason it doesn't work, then we can go back and say it's one of two things. It's either the list or it's the sales copy. It's one of those two things, because we know the funnel works so it's one of the other two elements that's getting them there or not getting them there. So it really depends on the niche and the type of offer to determine whether or not you test it out online first.

BEN SETTLE: Do you have a lot of experience renting your own list to other companies and how that works?

CRAIG SIMPSON: Sure. The thing I like to do is I prefer to have a list broker manage it for me. It's like a listing agent for real estate. The way it works is they put it on the market for you, they market it, they let other people know that it's available for rent, and then they usually get around 20% of the rental income.

Just for easy numbers let's say you rent it for $100 for every 1,000 names that somebody else rents from you. If that's the case and somebody rents 1,000 names, you're going to get $80 and the list broker is going to get $20, but the reality is the list broker that manages it is really only going to get $10 because $10 is going to go to them and $10 is going to go to the broker that brought the renter to them. They split that commission. So, it's your $80 and then the two list brokers split $20.

BEN SETTLE: Is there a minimum number that you can rent a list out for, as far as how many thousands of people on it?

CRAIG SIMPSON: If you're going to put up 1,500 names a year, that's probably not enough. If you were to put up 1,500 names a quarter then you probably have enough to put on the market. If it's 1,500 prospects, that probably isn't going to work. You need to have at least 1,500 buyers to make available.

Now, in some case inquiry or prospect lists can work, but you need to have a higher volume of them. You need to have a minimum of 3,000 or 5,000 per quarter in order for the list to get enough rentals on them.

BEN SETTLE: The question that I wanted to ask you in the beginning and it just kind of slipped my mind because I wanted to get right into the meat is how did you get into this direct mail world, just your own personal experience?

CRAIG SIMPSON: I got into it in a really weird way. When I was about 18 or 19 I got really heavily involved in rock climbing and I built this 20' high rock climbing wall in my backyard. When I got done building it I didn't have any money left over to buy the fake rock climbing holds that you bolt onto the wall, so I thought, "Well, I'll make my own," and I found this weird recipe to make my own rock climbing holds.

My friends loved it and they were climbing on my wall with my fake rocks on there and thought it was so cool, and they were like, "You should try selling these." I thought, "Hey, that's kind of cool, I'll do that," so I went into business for myself selling these fake rock climbing holds.

On my first mailing, I mailed out to 250 people. I selected all the addresses, I hand-wrote the envelopes, I put the postage stamp on myself, the whole nine yards, and sat by the phone and thought I was going to be killed with orders. The phone didn't ring one time. It was a complete bomb, but I didn't give up. I kept on trying and I eventually found some systems that worked and I sold over 4,000 rocks through the mail. I was really green and really rough, but I made it work.

I hated the manufacturing part of the business. The phone would ring and I'd be excited because my marketing was working at the time, but I hated going out to my own sweatshop where I'd actually build these things. I was working with polyester resins and sand and all this stuff and I was miserable, so I sold that company.

Then I took the little experience I had and it got me a job with a large financial publisher called the Ken Roberts company, and they educated me even more and got me to the next level. I got to the point where I was mailing 20-30 million sales pieces a year, setting up really sophisticated back-end sales funnels and all sorts of stuff.

So that was my start. It started with selling rocks through the mail. Then I went into financial publishing, and then about eight or nine years ago I came out on my own and have been doing freelance direct mail ever since then.

BEN SETTLE: That's very, very cool. Now the most important question is where can people find out more about you and the awesome course I've been going through that you sell, and your newsletter and your services and anything else you want to talk about.

CRAIG SIMPSON: Thank you. The thing is there are a lot of small business owners out there who want to try and do direct mail themselves and they're not sure how to go about it, so I put together a few resources to make it much easier for them.

I have a course called "Million Dollar Direct Mail System," and it literally takes you from A to Z and educates you on how to put a complete direct mail campaign together. It talks about picking lists, how to write copy, how to track the campaign, how to set up a back-end sales funnel with follow-up for the campaign – it's everything A to Z. If you go to my website at www.simpson-direct.com, there's a tab that says Direct Mail Course. You can go on there and you can read all about the course and you can order it online there.

I also have a newsletter called the Mailbag Millionaire newsletter. It's a monthly newsletter subscription that gives you all the tips, techniques, and latest trends in direct mail. I mail that out monthly.

Both those items are great for the advanced direct mail guy or the beginner. I have a lot of big name marketing gurus who subscribe to my newsletter because they love the content. I also ask guys who are just getting started to subscribe to it because they love how it educates them and teaches them the tips for direct mail marketing.

I would love for anybody who's interested if they want to find out more just go to my website at www.simpson-direct.com and there's all sorts of stuff on there that can help you out – tools and tips and a blog and all sorts of stuff.

BEN SETTLE: Great, man. I can't thank you enough for doing this. I really appreciate it. I've been kind of bragging about how I get to talk to you today, so it's been fun. It's actually a very big deal and this has been extremely helpful and I really appreciate it.

CRAIG SIMPSON: Great. I hope everyone gets a lot out of it, and I really appreciate you taking the time to interview me. I really do hope it's a benefit to your subscribers.

BEN SETTLE: I'm sure it will be. Thanks again for your time, Craig. Bye now.

Chapter 10
How to Use Contests
to Quickly Pack *Thousands*
of New Subscribers
onto Your Email List

BEN SETTLE: Today I'm talking with Josh Earl — who is an "Email Players" subscriber. Josh, you've built a sizeable list using contests, but before we get into all that tell us what your business is and what you do and a little bit about your background.

Josh Earl: Sure. I'm a programmer. That's my full-time job, and over the last couple of years I got into ebook publishing. I just kind of learned about it online, read a couple of interesting articles, and on a whim just decided to publish a book of my own based off a blog post I did that got a lot of traffic. That actually sold pretty well when I first launched it, $2,000 to $3,000 on that, so from there I've pretty much just continued to promote that book and a follow-up book that I wrote. They're both books for programmers about using a particular programming tool.

Meanwhile I was still doing my day job and kind of falling in love with marketing. I've been studying marketing a lot, very much learning as I go. I had my product first and it wasn't really based on any kind of audience research, so I got lucky with it, but I've managed to turn it into some nice steady income. I've probably earned at this point about $30,000 from it over the last two years, just kind of feeling my way through things.

BEN SETTLE: Tell us the story about how you used contests to build things. It was pretty impressive, the numbers you were telling me. Can you tell us how all that came about and how big the list was and the quality of the list and whatever else you want to add to it?

Josh Earl: Sure. I'll back up a little bit here. Pretty much I've used Twitter to grow my email list from the outset. I learned about email marketing shortly before I published my first book. I kept reading, "The money's in the list," so I was like, "All right, then I should probably start collecting some email addresses."

I started using Twitter by starting up a content curation feed where I retweeted interesting stuff that I found that I thought my audience would be interested in. I just kind of gradually grew that Twitter account over the last couple of years. Before I did this contest I'd gotten it up to about 13,000 followers, which on social media is decent but you're not going to get a lot of sales off of that, but I figured out that I could use that Twitter account to constantly drive people back to my email list.

Several times a week I would tweet invitations to join my mailing list and send people over to my landing page. After doing that for a while I got to thinking that maybe I could get some more people interested if I did a giveaway.

The tool that my book is about is called Sublime Text. It's a text editor for programmers and it costs about $70. There's a lot of people who use it who just haven't paid for it yet because you can use it as a free trial, so I decided to do a giveaway to give away a free license of that.

My first giveaway was about six months after I published my book. I had a few thousand Twitter followers and I ran the giveaway for about 10 days and I just tweeted about it every day. People got kind of annoyed and some of them unfollowed me, but it worked really well actually. From where I was sitting at the time, I think I grew my list by about 400 email signups, which for me was great. I think I had just a few hundred people on my list at the time, so I realized the giveaway idea had some legs to it.

Typically, I would run a giveaway like this, and then I would turn around shortly after that and do a sale on my book. The first time I got a nice little handful of sales, so I decided to do it again about six months later. I think I did this last November, right before Cyber Monday, so I was planning to do another giveaway and then roll right into a Cyber Monday sale off of that.

I wrote up a blog post about the giveaway this time and I published that. Then I posted that up on Hacker News, which is a programmer website that gets a fair amount of traffic. It took off on Hacker News and I got a bunch of traffic off of that.

BEN SETTLE: With the Hacker News was that a paid ad or how did you get it up there?

Josh Earl: No, it's kind of like Digg. It's a social link-sharing type of thing, so if people are interested in it they'll upvote it, and if they upvote enough times you hit the home page. If you hit the home page you can get like 20,000 to 30,000 hits on your website in just a few hours. It's a pretty decent amount of traffic, but it's very hit or miss. You can't really bank on it. For the second giveaway that I did last year I managed to get my blog post about the giveaway up on Hacker News and it hit the front page, so I ended up getting a lot of traffic from that.

Between the Hacker News traffic and then my constant tweeting about it – I ran it for about a week and I tweeted about it a couple times a day – between those two I ended up getting about 1,400 email signups and I was ecstatic. That was probably another 30% added to my list at that point.

But one thing really bugged me when I was doing these contests. It seemed like it was just fundamentally flawed because I was basically asking people to do something that was against their best interests, or I was hoping they would do something against their best interests, and programmers are pretty savvy so they would figure this out pretty quickly.

What I was hoping is that they would enter the contest by joining my email list, but then that they would also share about my contest either through Twitter, Facebook, or upvoting on Hacker News so that I'd get more traffic. But the more people that entered, the less chance anyone had to win, so if you thought about it for a minute you'd be like, "Why would anyone share?" If you're in a lottery with 10 people and you tell an 11th person, now you have 10% less chance to win, and I think people were smart enough to figure this out. So, I got some decent traffic, but I didn't get explosive results out of it.

Fast forward to this summer. I was thinking about doing another giveaway a couple months ago, but that conflict of interest just bugged me and I couldn't think of a way to deal with it. One day I got an email from a guy who's pretty well-known in the programmer community. There's a company called AppSumo and the founder of that is Noah Kagan and he sent an email out to his list with a giveaway on it.

I didn't think anything of it at the time. I just kind of archived it and then I was like, "Oh, you know what, let me unarchive that and check it out. Noah's pretty sharp. This might be interesting," so I took a look at it and I ended up entering the contest. He had some Seth Godin books that he was giving away, so I entered the contest. Then my jaw hit the floor when I saw what he was doing.

When I entered the contest, I got basically an affiliate link. He didn't call it that. He called it a lucky URL. What this URL does is if I were to share it and then my friends were to enter the contest using that URL, I would get more entries. So, it kind of takes that self-interest problem that I had before, flips it on its head, and now suddenly you've got all these people who are dying to share your links because it helps them.

He was running the giveaway with a WordPress plugin so I immediately tracked it down and bought it and that weekend I set up another Sublime license giveaway. I threw this contest together in about two hours. I had to write a couple emails to go with it. At the time, I had about 13,000 Twitter followers and about 5,500 email subscribers, so a decent little list but not huge.

So, I put this contest together and it was pretty much just a matter of installing this plugin and configuring it. There were a few little things to set up. I threw a screen shot of the software in there, and I wrote an email to send to my list and scheduled a bunch of tweets. I have a Twitter scheduler tool that I use, so I was going to promote it every day. I decided to run it for 11 days and promote it every day on Twitter.

I got it all set up Sunday morning and had it all scheduled for 10 am on Monday morning. The email went out at 10 am and then I immediately got just a barrage of emails back from people telling me that the link was broken.

BEN SETTLE: At least you know they're reading. [laughing]

Josh Earl: Yes, exactly. [laughing] I was like, "Oh crap," so I fixed the link and re-sent the email, then I just tried to forget about the whole thing. I was too stressed out about it so I just went back to work. I'm an iOS programmer so I went back to doing some coding.

Finally, 8 pm rolls around and I get up the courage to log into Google Analytics like, "Is anybody paying attention to this thing?" and I took a look and I had at that very moment almost 500 people on my website at once. I'd never seen more than 20 or 30, so my website is basically melting at this point, and I had more than 12,000 email addresses that I'd collected in the first 8 or 10 hours.

The contest basically went viral because people were sharing. My initial blast to my list got about 1,500 people to enter, then from there those people all shared the link to my contest, and it just rippled out from there. It was insane.

The guys that wrote the plugin had live stats so they could see. My plugin would phone home and they could kind of watch what was going on from their end. It was all over Twitter. I ended up getting almost 500,000 page views on my website over the course of the contest, which was 11 days, like I said.

There were definitely some people that were trying to game the system. There was one guy in particular who submitted 101,000 entries. This is what you get for marketing to programmers, because they figure out how to hack it. This guy just set up some kind of bot farm or something and was just hammering it, so I disqualified him and banned him. But it went nuts, and the viral effect of giving people an incentive to share the contest really floored me. I ended up growing my email list by 3,418%.

There were definitely some mixed results. There were definitely some people entering fake addresses, like I mentioned, but the majority of them seemed to be really legit. I think the legit addresses ended up coming to around 120,000. I think I had around 169,000 total, and I just imported the entire thing. I actually broke this plugin that these guys had written. I had too many optins and I couldn't export them from WordPress.

BEN SETTLE: That's a good problem to have, man.

Josh Earl: It's a great problem to have, yeah, so they had to rewrite parts of the plugin to make it so that I could even download the thing. So, I downloaded the whole thing as a CSV file, imported it into MailChimp, and from there I announced the results of the contest, which was really interesting, if you've never sent 189,000 emails. I didn't know what to expect. I was kind of prepared for the worst.

There were definitely a lot of troll-ish people. I got a handful of emails back from people who were mad. I think there were some people who thought I was giving away a free license to everybody that entered, which I did the numbers and it would have cost me like $11 million, like they thought I was Oprah Winfrey or something, so there were some people that were really mad about it. But there were a lot more people like the guy who told me I restored his faith in humanity because he thought he was just going to get spammed.

The way I handled it was I kind of said, "Hey, you're getting email from me now. Here's the contest winner. If you don't want to get any more emails from me, please scroll to the bottom and unsubscribe now and I won't bother you anymore."

BEN SETTLE: Very good idea. Seriously, I'm glad you did that. The reason I'm bringing that out is for people who are reading this transcript. I think that's a great way if you add a bunch of names, especially from a mass advertising thing. I love to do stuff like that. You want to get the lukewarm and cold people off.

Josh Earl: Exactly. I don't know where I got that idea from. [laughing]

BEN SETTLE: I just like the simplicity of how you did that, I really do.

Josh Earl: I definitely got that from listening to you. So, I invited people to unsubscribe and I cleaned out the list pretty quickly. I had about 23,000 bounces that were just bad addresses. Then I had a bunch of people unsubscribe, but not as many as you'd think. I think it was like 6% total.

BEN SETTLE: That's not bad at all.

Josh Earl: No. Actually, I got my hand slapped from MailChimp for my high unsubscribe rate for that one particular email, but it wasn't as bad as I feared, and I had fun. Some of the people who emailed me back were swearing at me and stuff, and I had some fun. I replied to a few of them just to kind of push back so I felt like a man, then I just started unsubscribing people. Anybody who's like, "Where's my free license?" I just unsubscribed all of them, no messing around.

So I did that, and then I've sent out several other kind of follow-up emails. Most of them have been just straight content for now because I'm treating these as really, really cold leads that I want to warm up before I try to pitch too much.

BEN SETTLE: By the way, you're playing with fire doing that. I know that's not what the call is about, but just unsolicited advice, I admit it. It doesn't have to be anything expensive. It doesn't really even have to be something that they buy, but make sure they have some skin in the game because they're going to turn on you.

The angry ones that you've already gotten, it's going to be way worse than that because they're expecting free stuff from you at this point. Maybe at least refer them to a product, even if you're not selling it, just something so that they get that mindset. It doesn't even have to be something you're selling, like I said. You could just recommend a product and say, "Look, I don't get paid anything for this," but just get them in the habit of clicking links that you send them, that's all.

Josh Earl: I like that idea. There's some affiliate stuff I could do.

BEN SETTLE: That would be much better to actually get paid, but just something. Use the system and just make it fun for them, maybe a special bonus if they buy from your affiliate link, that they can't get anywhere else. Anyway, I didn't want to derail you here.

Josh Earl: That's okay, good advice. So I've gotten it cleaned out and I'm going to send out a couple more emails probably and then just delete everybody who hasn't opened anything. Right now it's looking like it's going to end up right around 80,000.

BEN SETTLE: That's not bad, man. I'll be interested to hear how responsive they are when you do sell them, because if this turns out to be a responsive list, you've hit a gold mine, man.

Josh Earl: I think so. I did do an experimental mailing to about 1,000. I moved about 1,000 of them into an autoresponder sequence where I sent them two content emails and then a pitch basically, just as an experiment, and I didn't get any blowback from it. I didn't get as many sales as I was hoping for, but I did get about 14 sales out of that so it was a decent enough response that I think that I'll be able to use this list. It's not a bunch of deadbeats I don't think.

The people that I'm keeping are all people that have already kind of raised their hand a little bit by opening the email and not unsubscribing, so I'm expecting to get at least some really decent attention early on from this list over the next few weeks.

In the meantime I've been talking about this with some of my friends, and I've actually kind of coached a couple of other people informally to set up and run their own giveaways. Some of them had really tiny lists, just a couple hundred people. One guy that basically took my entire giveaway and copied it almost word-for-word – you could almost say he swiped it – I think he had just a couple hundred people and he ended up getting 140 people out of it, which isn't fabulous but for him it was a big win.

It seems like it's definitely proportionate to the size of your audience. If you've got a few hundred people, I'm seeing people tending to double, just another 100% on top of what they already have. One guy I know had I think around 1,500 to 2,000 people and he got close to doubling his list. He got around 2,000.

Then another guy that I know had around 1,000. He was smarter and he reached out to a bunch of people on Twitter who had a lot of followers and got them to tweet about his giveaway, and he ended up getting at least 3,000. I think he tripled his list. I'm seeing it working for a lot of people, so it's a pretty interesting idea to play with.

For me one of the big takeaways is that the offer that you make is really, really important in terms of who you're going to end up attracting. I've seen people do giveaways before, and if you don't do it right you're going to end up with garbage. I've seen people do giveaways for a Kindle Fire or an iPad or a Macbook or something, and you're going to get everybody and their grandma because that stuff is not specific. Everybody would want that stuff.

The giveaway that I did was very specific to my audience. Only programmers who use this one tool would even care about this giveaway at all. Similarly, the people that I've been coaching, a lot of them will do kind of an ebook collection for a bunch of programming books that are all related to one specific topic, and that's working well and getting them good attention and some good traction with their particular audience.

So that's kind of what I've done.

BEN SETTLE: I think that's pretty cool, man. Do you have any other just random tips that you can think of for someone who's reading this and they're like, "Man, I'd like to try that." What advice would you give someone who just wants to try it really quick? Maybe they can't do it exactly how you're doing it, but they want to try it just to see if it works for them.

Josh Earl: My first couple of contests I did were really crude. I wrote a blog post, tweeted a link to that blog post, threw an optin form on the bottom of it, and that was it. I just did a drawing from my mailing list. I just exported that to Excel and just picked a name from there, so you can do it with very little set-up.

One thing that's really important, particularly if you're going to try to go for this viral approach, it's really, really important to get that initial push. If you don't have enough of an audience to give it that push yourself, then you need to do some thinking ahead of time and find some people who can help you out. That might influence your choice of what you give away.

If you can find a piece of software that's really interesting to people, or somebody who has a big audience – like I mentioned Kagan gave away Seth Godin's books and he was hoping he'd get some love from Seth Godin, which would have been huge. I think that didn't end up happening, but if you can partner with somebody ahead of time and promote their stuff and then get them to promote your contest, that will go a long way towards getting it going. Then from there it can become self-sustaining.

BEN SETTLE: That's a really good idea. Have you ever played with giving multiple things away – not just one thing to one person but maybe 10 winners?

Josh Earl: No, I haven't, but that's a good idea, especially if you can work with multiple vendors and get several prizes. One giveaway I know about, they gave away lifetime licenses to Dropbox. If you can get two or three of those, Dropbox already has a big audience, so if you can get a couple other big software companies to give away licenses – LeadPages is another one that's popular with the internet marketing crowd, so if you can give away a license to that and a couple other marketing-related things, for example, and you can get all of them promoting your giveaway at once, you can get a lot of cross-traffic that way.

BEN SETTLE: That's really cool. You said you were coaching some friends. If someone's reading this and they want to learn from you, can they pay you to coach them on this? Have you thought about doing that?

Josh Earl: Yeah, I have.

BEN SETTLE: I didn't know if you were doing it that way or if you were just doing it for friends.

Josh Earl: I'd welcome that. I've been doing it for my friends up until now, but if somebody wants to hit me up I'd be willing to talk to them.

BEN SETTLE: How can they contact you? What's the best way?

Josh Earl: The best way would probably to go to my blog, which is www.joshuaearl.com and there's a contact form on there. Then I did get a discount code for the plugin that I used. If people go to www.joshuaearl.com/emailplayers there's going to be an optin form there, and if you opt in I will send you a discount code that's good for 50% off this plugin. The plugin costs $197 normally, but it will be $97 with that code.

The whole contest cost me $97 for the plugin, then $70 for the license, so I've spent at this point far more in email service provider costs. I think it cost me $700 or $800 to import all these into MailChimp. The contest itself was pennies per name, if that.

BEN SETTLE: This is good, man. I really appreciate you taking the time on a Saturday to share all this and for telling me about it in the first place. It's been great, man. I really appreciate it.

Josh Earl: Thanks for the opportunity. Saturday is the day I work on my own stuff instead of working for the man.

BEN SETTLE: And here's some more unsolicited advice, since you asked for it. The first hour of every day should belong to you.

Josh Earl: I have listened to that episode that you guys did about that two or three times. I spend about an hour and a half to two hours every morning doing that, and I've been doing that for a while.

BEN SETTLE: Oh, you're good to go. You'll be out of that situation before you know it. Thank you again for your time today.

Chapter 11
How to Make Facebook
Your List Building Bitch

BEN SETTLE: Shane, before we got into all the stuff I want to ask you, tell us a little bit about yourself. Email Players are a skeptical lot, trained so by me to not trust anybody, so who are you and what are you about?

SHANE HUNTER: I can read the excerpt from the book that I'm writing right now to kind of give you the background on me. "I wasn't always this ambitious. There was a time when I was a record-label-seeking poor-as-hell musician with no money, no hope, and no ambition. All I had to my name was a 1980's Dodge minivan with faded light blue paint and a pinhole leak in the gas tank. In that van was literally everything that I had, which was basically a few pairs of clothes, a bunch of instruments and recording equipment, and some bedding. Okay, so I'm lying. There were also a few Canadian dimes and pennies on the floor of that rusty old $300 van." That's kind of where I came from. I'm from Canada originally. I moved to the US to be in a band that fell apart for one reason or another – that reason being I ended up marrying my bandmate's girlfriend. A couple years ago I started digging into internet marketing and got good at a few disciplines, mostly being traffic and lead generation, and that's kind of my story.

BEN SETTLE: That's cool. So you talk about traffic and lead generation, which is exactly what I want to talk about, as you know. You and I were hanging out in Carlsbad. My dad got a kick out of listening to us talk because we were trying to compete on who works less hours. I think you won that. What is your specialty now? Do you have one or two things you're especially good at, or is it everything?

SHANE HUNTER: Really my specialty is being able to split test and actually look at data. It's not one specific type of traffic. Learning that strategy has enabled me to go into any type of traffic generation that I want to and do really well with it as soon as I figure out the fine details of it.
What I've been known for for the last couple of years was actually search engine optimization, SEO, but I've purposely been pushing myself to go more and more into

paid traffic, specifically because Google is kind of a big dirty bitch. They're not friends of anybody that's an affiliate or that's an internet marketer, and the list goes on and on. They've been slapping people since 2008, and it's only getting worse. It's still doable, but because of that inconsistency I started moving into other areas.

BEN SETTLE: The question that everybody asks – they don't ask me because they know I have no clue – but is SEO dead or is it just something that's dying or is it just changing? Do people still worry about it?

SHANE HUNTER: As someone who's been doing SEO for way too long, there's probably nothing that makes you cringe you more than "SEO is dead" as a phrase. It's never dead. You have to understand that it's a computer program, so it takes the variables that you give it, it processes them, and it makes a computation and comes up with the equation. As such, it will always be gameable. The key is to find out what variables they're looking for, and then you will always be able to game a computer program, the same way that it works with Facebook, the same way that it works with Google. It's just an algorithm, which is a mathematical formula saying $A + B + C =$ money.

BEN SETTLE: I had this talk with Jim Yaghi. He doesn't claim to be Mr. SEO but he has this thing he calls reverse SEO, which I always thought was interesting. Have you ever heard me talk about that?

SHANE HUNTER: I haven't.

BEN SETTLE: I'm going to try to give what I think he was saying. I'll probably butcher this a little, but you'll probably get it. I had to ask him recently, "Is this still applicable?" and he said, "Yes." What he'll do is go into Google Analytics and he'll say, "Look at the keywords that Google is sending people to your site with. Then don't necessarily keyword-stuff anything or care about keywords, but just write about that topic on your blog." Is that still a pretty good way to do it, because that seems pretty simple to me. I like that.

SHANE HUNTER: That's really a good way. It's kind of a good and a bad, because as we talked about, I like to work as little as possible, so if they're already coming for those keywords, why the hell am I trying to go more into that? It gives you a relevance factor, seeing those keywords, but at the same time they're already coming to your site for those keywords. Typically, I would look for new keywords that aren't being touched that you're more interested in writing about.

I never particularly write for SEO because on-page SEO has actually become less of a factor over the last two years. Their PR department tries to tell you that it's all about high-quality content and that sort of thing, but you've seen huge sites butchered that are nothing but content, that aren't using any sort of black hat strategies or anything along those lines. My advice to people, when you're writing for SEO, write about what you're good at, what can offer value and help your target market, and then just things that are controversial, as you and I know how to do.

BEN SETTLE: I should probably clarify something that Jim was teaching with that, because I know what you're saying. He was like, "When you do that, Google will show you more keywords that people are finding that aren't the same, then you just keep writing articles and content about the subjects, not necessarily even using those words. Then it just keeps giving you new things, and it's telling you exactly what it wants you to write about." That's how I interpret it, at least.

SHANE HUNTER: It gives you all sorts of long-tails that you can do. I think that plays more of a factor when you're in a smaller specific niche, like say you're the internet marketing pay per click guy. You really only have a small list of things that you can write about at any given time, so that's why it's good to kind of rehash and go for the long tail and write derivatives of that original article that created those keywords. I can definitely see the value in doing that. Another trick if you really want to find related terms to your topic – so you've done a little bit of keyword research and you find some sort of keyword like *email newsletter* – like say you were trying to promote via SEO Email Players, so you wanted to rank for *email newsletter.* If you go to Google and type in *email newsletter*, at the very bottom of that first page, generally speaking there's a list of related searches. There's usually anywhere from 5-10 related searches that have to do with *email newsletter,* so you can target those. This is like the pre-emptive version of what Jim Yaghi is teaching with that reverse SEO.

BEN SETTLE: Since you're kind of moving away from SEO it sounds like, what's your favorite traffic method?

SHANE HUNTER: Right now it's definitely Facebook, simply because you can pick your target market down to whether they like to eat peanut butter sandwiches. You can target people that in the next 6 months are in the market to buy a Mercedes Benz. It's never been so specific, unless you're really going into heavy direct mail stuff, but online I feel like there's never been an opportunity like there is with what Facebook is doing. Even though everyone's sketching out about Facebook right now because of the possibility of being banned, that possibility is there with any network that you're ever in. I just look at the amount of data that they've collected. There's a reason that they're worth so bloody much, and it's because of the data. That data to me is a marketer's best friend.

BEN SETTLE: It's kind of foolish to rely just on one thing anyway, in any avenue. What is that Dan Kennedy-ism? One is the most dangerous number?

SHANE HUNTER: Yeah, exactly. This is why with Facebook I'll also add in Bing pay per click and Google pay per click – although Google pay per click I'm not a huge fan of, just because the competition is so high, which drives up your prices. Again, I'm a huge metrics guy. I keep my costs as low as possible, while not freaking out about paying a large amount. If it's making you profit then go for it, but I like to minimize those costs and maximize the money that I'm bringing in. It just kind of makes sense. As such, I can get a bunch of traffic from Bing. Like I said, I still do use Google pay per click, just not as much because of the prices.

BEN SETTLE: Let's go back to Facebook, since that's your favorite. What are some tips you have? We're talking to people here who are like me. We don't know jack about any of this. Get as infantile as you need to in explaining this. How do we get going with Facebook in a way where we have a good foundation and we're doing it right? You can never totally not be banned someday, who knows, but what advice would you give to your own family member who needed help to get started on Facebook? What would you tell them?

SHANE HUNTER: Don't play with guns in the dark. By that I mean create your customer avatar. One of the biggest things that I see with coaching a whole lot of people on traffic and lead generation and that sort of thing is you have these people who are like, "Yeah! I'm going to do pay per click! It's going to be f-ing awesome!" and they go out and do it and they broadcast like old school television or old school newspaper where there's no specific target in mind. They're just like, "Hey! I'm selling hot tubs" when it might be somebody that already owns a hot tub or it might be someone that doesn't give a crap about hot tubs or someone that's allergic to hot tubs, and that's a lot of wasted money – a lot of wasted money. The more refined you can create your customer avatar, the better. Like for you, I would pick your favorite winery and then I would try to sell you wine from that winery. It seems like a pretty good plan – make sure that you're in the market for buying wine, make sure that you like this specific type of wine, etc. With Facebook, you can really target down to crazy, crazy levels.

The second piece of advice there is don't be dumb. By that I mean don't be ignorant and pretend that you know what your customer is thinking better than they do. One of the biggest things I've done with all sorts of advertising and all sorts of traffic is to split test. You might say, "This customer avatar that I created is going to rock," and then you'll do it and you'll find out it flops. That's not because you did something wrong. It was just an incorrect guess. If you split test and you find three or four different customer avatars that you think are a right fit for your product, and test those against each other, you're going to find a clear winner almost every single time. Then from there you just keep on further refining that customer avatar until it's fine-tooth comb details that you're targeting your customers with. Then you get maximum ROI for the least amount of money possible, because Facebook is going to lower the price for your ads because more people are clicking on it, or you can do cost per action, or you can do cost per 1,000 views. The point is, because they're more relevant, Facebook is going to lower those prices, plus they're going to convert higher because you found the right audience.

BEN SETTLE: That's really good information. So, taking it back even more infantile, do they just have like a button you push on Facebook if you want to start advertising? Is it pretty simple to get started in it? How does that work?

SHANE HUNTER: It really is. I think it's like the left sidebar when you go in. This is when you're on a desktop computer. You can't do this from a phone. On the left hand side, there's something like "Create an ad" or "Open an ad account." I don't remember from the first time because it's been a few years, but it's something to that effect. "Advertise here!" It's advertising, so it's pretty easy to find.

BEN SETTLE: So that part, even if they change it, we'll know where to find it.

SHANE HUNTER: Right. And if you can't find it, go to Google and in every browser that exists, in the top right corner usually there's a little search box, so even if you don't know how to Google, go to that and type in 'how to start an advertising account on Facebook' or 'how to open an ad account on Facebook' or something along those lines, and you will find the answer there. That's one of the biggest things that I teach anybody that I ever mentor or teach, is learn to use Google. You have the oracle or the great library sitting at your fingertips, and most people don't use it.

BEN SETTLE: So you're still using Google when you're doing Facebook ads, basically.

SHANE HUNTER: Yes, because Google is an endless supply of knowledge. If there's something that you're stuck on, in a couple of minutes of searching you can usually find the answer. Don't let yourself get caught up in chasing information and not taking action, because that's also one of the banes of people that are starting out.

BEN SETTLE: I assume it's pretty simple to just put an ad up. That's probably pretty self-explanatory when they get in there. Is there anything they should know, or I should know, if I'm going to go in there?

SHANE HUNTER: Basically you're going to need images, because as you know with copy, the first thing that you're doing with a Facebook ad is a pattern interrupt. If it blends in to everything else that's there, nobody's going to see it, but also if it looks like a 2-year-old drew it – depending on your target market – it might not look professional enough. For images, I'm lucky because I've dinked around with everything in internet marketing, from graphic design to web design to coding to traffic to copywriting and everything in-between, so I'm good enough at Photoshop that I can make ads that work really well. If you can't do that, go to Fiverr.com and you can find graphic designers for $5 that will create an image for your ad. Everything else is self-explanatory. There's a whole Frequently Asked Questions, walkthroughs etc in the background of Facebook in their advertising office. If those don't answer your questions, you can always Google specific questions you might have.

BEN SETTLE: You talked about how it's a pattern interrupt. Speaking just for images, what tips do you have for that? If they were going to design their own, or if they wanted to give instructions to someone on Fiverr, what are some good ways to do a pattern interrupt, or does it differ with every market?

SHANE HUNTER: It kind of depends on the market you're going for. For example, today we're promoting an affiliate program called MOBE – My Online Business Empire, and it teaches people how to make money with online type stuff, not a big deal. I literally just started this today with some of the ads that I created. The customer avatar that I created was after doing a bunch of research. I went to Alexa.com, and what that does is give you a bunch of data and demographic info on websites. I went and plugged in the affiliate program's website to Alexa.com and it told me that it was predominantly males between 30-50 years old, in the United States or Australia, so that's a pretty good start already to break it down for what my customer avatar is. Now I've just eliminated a whole bunch of people.

Now, thinking about these people that are the type that are looking for extra income and that sort of thing, I started looking into what sort of entertainment are these guys into? What resonates with these sorts of people? So I started going to websites like

Nielson. Their whole job is to tear apart the demographic information for television shows. I started looking at the different television stations that fit my customer avatar. I was looking for stations that were predominantly watched by males between 30-50, that had an average income of $50,000 or more, and that sort of detail. I found four or five different TV stations that fit that profile really, really well.

Then I started looking at the programming that they had, the TV shows that they had and the movies that they would play. One of the ones that I found that I actually really like is Office Space. So I jump back to Facebook and in the targeting – which is all self-explanatory in the back office – I went and found the people who meet that criteria. They were males only from the United States, between 30-50 years old, they make $50,000 or more per year, and then the add-on that I did was they had to like the movie Office Space. This gave me a list of 110,000 people to start putting my ad out to. I do not suggest doing what I'm doing, but I'm a little bit more bold than the average bear. I created a bunch of advertisements that used screen shots from the movie Office Space.

BEN SETTLE: Which could be potentially a copyright problem?

SHANE HUNTER: Oh, absolutely. You can get your ass handed to you for doing that. That's why I say I do not advocate doing this, but it is an idea. Another thing you can do if you don't want to be that bold is you can say – as you know with copywriting – 'yes framing' in the ad. "Do you like The Office Space?" and get them to say yes that first time. Then they're like, "Wait, what does this have to do with The Office Space?" and then ask, "Do you hate your job too?" "Hell yeah, I do." "Well, here's what I found that helps me so I don't have to work my shitty job anymore, and I don't have to put up with my boss anymore."

BEN SETTLE: So you walk them right through all their hot buttons and interests and all that in one little ad.

SHANE HUNTER: Exactly, and that's what's nice about targeting down to something like a movie or TV show. It gives you that edge, because you already know that they like Office Space. It's like they told you that personally through that data, because at some point in their life they clicked Like on the Office Space Facebook page. I know that going in so I can make that assumption, and then I can do that 'yes frame.' Then I know what that movie or that TV show is about, so I can say, "Do you hate your job?" because there's a good chance that they do – and if they don't, then they're not in the right market for a money-making opportunity anyway, so who cares.

BEN SETTLE: But you've looked at other parts of their make-up, so it's not just a TV show anyway.

SHANE HUNTER: Exactly. That's just the icing on the cake. These ads are really simple. It just says, "Work less, play more, enjoy life." Have you seen the movie?

BEN SETTLE: I have not seen it, no.

SHANE HUNTER: They take this photocopier thing that keeps on giving them an error message, and "PC load letter" is the error message. People who have seen it know that phrase. One of the scenes is the three guys take this copier out into the middle of a field and just beat the shit out of it mercilessly with a baseball bat and stomp it and all that sort of thing. It's like quintessential office worker rage. Then another one is a screen shot of the actual scene in the movie where it reads "PC load letter" on the copier itself. Then in another one is like the perfect archetype dickhead boss that's the kind of main antagonist in this movie. I took a screen shot of him where he's just looking kind of douchey with his cup of coffee, and it's from a scene where he's like, "Mmm, yeah, so I'm going to need you to come in on Sunday. Thanks."

It's one of those things where it resonates with people because somebody in an office at one point has said something that pissed them off in that condescending tone of, "Well, I don't care that your time is important. In fact, it's not, so you're coming in." It was like these emotional impacts that I knew would trigger these people into clicking the ad, but at the same time I framed these ads so that the people that it doesn't resonate with, that aren't interested in making money, that aren't sick of their job, that aren't looking for something else aren't going to care about it.

BEN SETTLE: What if they just like the movie? Do you think they're going to click on that?

SHANE HUNTER: They might, but I don't generally deal in 'mights.' I believe that it's framed enough that I'm not going to have too many people that are clicking on it just because they like the movie, because it's not advertising the movie. It's not really saying, "Click here for the movie Office Space" or anything along those lines. It's very specific in what it promotes with the actual words of the copy that go around the ad. With the image you get a headline and you get a description above the image and a description below the image, so in those I explain exactly what they would be clicking on.

BEN SETTLE: What you're talking about here is really interesting. What you just taught us basically is how to set a nice cool ad up, actually. Would it work for other niches too, besides just the work at home one?

SHANE HUNTER: You can do this with vitamins, you can do this with whatever, like weight loss. Let's say we jump to that one. You could do like The Biggest Loser. I guarantee there's a huge following for that on Facebook, so you target people that like The Biggest Loser. Then you're like, "Do you like Jillian Michaels? Have you ever thought about losing weight?" and jump into what your product is.

BEN SETTLE: It seems to me like with your image too – and I don't mean to derail the subject, but just a brain fart – it seems to me that without invading any copyright notices you could just have an image that references something from those shows.

SHANE HUNTER: Absolutely. You could do a treadmill or whatever. Basically, you're trying to do, as I said, a pattern interrupt that is something to do with that pain in their life. I think it was you that told me at one point – I can't remember the exact phrase, but basically you want to poke their pain.

BEN SETTLE: Yeah, you want to rub salt in it. First of all, you want to find out everything they're insecure about and then you want to rub salt in it. It sounds kind of mean and all that, but you're doing them a service in a sense. They're going to ignore you otherwise.

SHANE HUNTER: You need to bring up that pain if you're ever going to solve it for them.

BEN SETTLE: Yeah, that's the whole thing. I like to do it in a way where it sounds like kind of an asshole-ish thing to do, but really, it's not. You can apply that to these Facebook ads.

SHANE HUNTER: Yeah, absolutely. Really, you don't have to use television shows or movies or anything along those lines. It's really just finding something specific so that you can talk to them on a specific level like you're talking to a good friend.

BEN SETTLE: You wouldn't go up to someone around the water cooler and just say something generic. You'd probably say, "What was on that show?" or "Did you hear about that thing in the news?" or whatever.

SHANE HUNTER: "Did you catch the game last night?" and because you both live in say San Diego, you're probably talking about the San Diego Chargers or something along those lines, and not the Philadelphia Eagles or something along those lines. You know already, through process of elimination, that this is what's on their mind, so you can play with that, thanks to Facebook.

BEN SETTLE: "Did you hear that my favorite winery was almost consumed in flames down in Escondido, right by Shane Hunter's house?" and you just happened to live there. That would get your attention.

SHANE HUNTER: Imagine if I made an ad to you, Ben, where I mention your favorite winery and say, "This shit almost burned down. You should probably buy a case of wine, because we're not even in fire season yet."

BEN SETTLE: I almost did that when I heard about that, but I didn't think they'd have time to ship me anything if there really was a fire there.

SHANE HUNTER: You put a picture of a case of that wine with that message of the urgency of, "Oh shit, we might burn down and then you'll never have your favorite wine again."

BEN SETTLE: What's interesting about this is what you're talking about here is very sophisticated compared to the ads I'm seeing on there now. They're nothing like this.

SHANE HUNTER: They're stupid. There's so much that you can do. The key is, you have to be creative. I'm thankful that my partner that I do a lot of this with is also a former musician, so we're generally pretty creative guys and we like to not do what everybody else does, because it's boring. As you know with copywriting, when you fit in and you're boring, nobody cares.

BEN SETTLE: When you fit in, you don't stick out.

SHANE HUNTER: That's why we take these different twists, and there's unlimited variance. I don't even remember how many billion users are on Facebook, but I think there's over a billion of them, so this tells you how many possibilities there are for you to target.

BEN SETTLE: Obviously I don't know all this nearly as well as you or probably even a basic Facebook advertiser does, but what you're doing doesn't seem like it's going to get you in any trouble with the powers that be. You're not really doing anything controversial.

SHANE HUNTER: No, not at all, and you don't have to. Really, it's about influence. The same way that you would talk to somebody that you're trying to get to know at work or at a bar or if you're trying to hit on a girl or whatever, it's the same sort of thing. Mention something like, "Oh, you're wearing a green shirt." You sound like a retard but they go, "Yeah, I am," and it's more yes framing. "I couldn't help but notice that you have hair. That's hot." [laughing]

BEN SETTLE: It's really cool how you can do that just by targeting the stuff they're already saying they identify with. I didn't realize there was that much information and intel.

SHANE HUNTER: One of the funny things that I actually just thought of last night when I was doing a whole bunch of ads is one of the main points for this particular affiliate program that I'm in is they offer to pay for a luxury Mercedes once you make like 12 sales.

BEN SETTLE: Is this that MOBE thing?

SHANE HUNTER: Yeah.

BEN SETTLE: I'm familiar with that.

SHANE HUNTER: One of the things that I found out that you can target in Facebook – and this was just me playing around – go back there and make yourself familiar with that back office and play with the options, because what I found out last night is you can find people that are specifically in the market to buy a Mercedes in the next six months that fit the rest of your demographics. Now imagine if you told them, "Hey, instead of spending $60K+ on a car, what if I told you a way to earn it for free, and make money?" It's just those small little twists that you can play with. I'm not saying that everybody that's in the market for that Mercedes is going to be down with this, but there's a good chance you could at least sign up a few people just on that premise, because you know exactly what they're looking for, you know the pain in their life, and you can address it.

BEN SETTLE: And add some depth. I like that, man. That's really cool. What other tips do you have for Facebook advertising, some cool stuff that you've discovered or some stories about where you made some big breakthroughs? Anything interesting that sticks out in your head?

SHANE HUNTER: One thing actually that I just learned about from a friend of mine, who's actually speaking with you in Vegas here in two weeks, Greg Gomez, if you know him.

BEN SETTLE: I've never met the guy, but I definitely know who he is.

SHANE HUNTER: He's good, and he's scaling up to be like a $100 million marketing firm type thing, so he really knows his stuff at like the industrial level. So I asked him, "Dude, is there any way that I can build [inaudible] ads, because building these things one at a time and split testing each one of these interests takes a hell of a long time." He showed me a website called Qwaya.com. I think it's like $150/month, but they give you a free 30-day trial if you enter your credit card. It allows you to go in and pick all the different interests that you want, pick whether you want male or female, and all the exact same stuff you can do in the back office of Facebook, but it has this clever little checkbox that you can click, and then it will segment all of those interests or the gender or the age gaps, like if you do it in 5-year gaps.

Last night in 5 minutes I created 250 ads, but it segmented like age 25-30, 30-35, 35-40, all the way up to 55. Then it was targeting specific interests that I thought they might like. It's make money type stuff so I targeted *Rich Dad, Poor Dad,* the book, and *Think and Grow Rich.* But instead of lumping all of those things together and kind of, like I said, playing with guns in the dark, you're separating each one of those interests.

Now one of those is going to come screaming ahead, or maybe several of them will, but some of them are going to suck, so you can turn off the ones that suck but keep on ramping up the ones that are doing well. This tool allows you to build all of those ads kind of at once, instead of taking the next 90 years to make them.

BEN SETTLE: That's kind of cool.

SHANE HUNTER: So say you went to Fiverr and got 6 or 7 images. This will do all of those variations, trying it with each one of those images. The split testing possibilities are kind of endless with that, and it literally saved me days, if not weeks of creating all of those ads manually. That's one of those big aha sort of moments that I've had, just literally two days ago. I went in there and just absorbed everything that

that was capable of. I think I've rolled out close to 1,000 ads in the last [inaudible]. Like we've discussed, I don't like working that much, and that took me less than an hour.

BEN SETTLE: How long would that have normally taken you – weeks?

SHANE HUNTER: It wouldn't have been possible. I would have needed 50 employees and it would have taken them 6 months.

BEN SETTLE: And you were able to do it all in an hour because of this one tool. Damn, man, that's pretty cool, it really is.

SHANE HUNTER: When you combine this sort of thought process of being creative, getting to know your customer avatar, and then actually trying to gain some kind of rapport and influence with them by something that they like, basically you're just finding a mutual interest. If you don't know that movie, you're not going to be able to ask these questions. I guarantee you're going to be able to find something in common. Run with that and then frame it accordingly, just like you're building influence and rapport with somebody in person.

BEN SETTLE: I would hope they'd be able to find something. If not, then they're in the wrong market. They should know something. Everybody should know at least some of that stuff before they get into anything.

SHANE HUNTER: And if you don't, find out a movie that they really like and go watch it. It's going to take you two hours and now you'll be able to ask questions to help get you in their mind. When you combine that sort of stuff with tools like this that let you split test at that level, not making money with whatever business in whatever sector that you're in – you don't have excuses. If you're a handyman, you can find people that like Lowe's and Home Depot and DIY TV shows or that sort of thing, or that are in the market for home renovations in the next six months, any of that sort of stuff. If you're putting on local seminars, "Here's how to build a shed," to actually going out and building them the shed – you set up the proper funnel on the other side of this ad and it's done.

It's not like you need to be a genius to get this stuff done. It's just thinking about the person that you're actually talking to. I think that's one of the big factors that a lot of people miss out on when they're advertising, is you're really just talking to a person.

173

BEN SETTLE: What I like about what you're talking about here is this is all the stuff that all the top A-level copywriters do, too. They don't even worry about the frickin' product. They want to know the market. In fact, I had discussions with these guys earlier in my career and they got me thinking the way you're talking. It's like you're not building a bridge from your product to your prospect. You're building a bridge from your prospect to your product. I went into the golf market and I'd never even played golf before and I didn't even have the product in my hand, but I was able to write 90% of the ad just because I knew their avatar the way you're describing it. With Facebook ads, my gosh, it's crazy. That's awesome, man.

SHANE HUNTER: It's limitless what you can do. Just with this segment, people should be thankful that you do these interviews, man. This is literally like one of those $1,000 or $2,000 products that gurus would sell, it really is. I just went through a course actually that did less than what I just shared, and they charged $2,000.

BEN SETTLE: When is the Shane Hunter system of Facebook advertising ever going to come out? Is it ever going to be put in a product and packaged up?

SHANE HUNTER: I don't know. You know me, I don't like to work that much. [laughing]

BEN SETTLE: I know, I totally get it, but you do do coaching.

SHANE HUNTER: I do. I do coaching and mentoring and that sort of thing. That's kind of the gist. Right now I'm working on a book, and that's probably how I'm actually going to end up doing a lot of this stuff, is through books, not the internet marketing voodoo info products. I think I will start moving more into actually creating books, even if it's self-publishing through Amazon and that sort of thing, kind of like that sweet zombie book.

BEN SETTLE: Did you read that one?

SHANE HUNTER: I haven't yet but it's in the plan, man. As you can tell, I've been busy – retardedly busy. I read obsessively and haven't been able to read in like 6-8 months.

BEN SETTLE: In other words, I would be winning the "who works less" at the moment. [laughing]

SHANE HUNTER: This is basically because I'm almost changing industries, going from SEO to this sort of thing, but that's just kind of who I am. We talked about this too when we were in Carlsbad. When we're actually learning something it's like, "Full bore, let's learn this, let's get completely immersed," and then it's like, "Okay, now I can just relax because I'm better than most people at it."

BEN SETTLE: All you've got to do is excel at it. I've never heard anybody take Facebook advertising to the depth to which you're describing. I'm sure there's a lot more that you can talk about, but the depth you just went into was like, "Whoa, man!" I'm sitting here taking little notes on my pad here. I usually write questions I'm going to ask, and I'm sitting here writing down what you're saying.

SHANE HUNTER: See, that's the good thing. That's what Email Players has done for me, too.

BEN SETTLE: It's all about traffic and conversion.

If somebody wanted to hire you as a coach or for mentoring, where can they contact you?

SHANE HUNTER: Probably the best place would be through Facebook on my fan page, which is just **www.Facebook.com/readshanehunter**. That's where I'm establishing the fan base for the books that I've got in the works, as well as any products that I actually do decide to create. They'll all come through there.

BEN SETTLE: That's cool. I think you're going to get a lot of people who are interested in knowing how to do this. It's very good. Any other last thoughts you want to leave with us before we wrap this up?

SHANE HUNTER: Go and do shit. [laughing] Just go and do shit. Stop worrying about, "Oh, I don't know if I have it all figured out." I didn't either, and that's how I got good at it. That's how Ben got good at everything that he does. We just did it. You get up and you do it. You fall a couple of times and it sucks. Worst case scenario you might lose a couple hundred or a couple thousand dollars, but you can bounce back from that because the stuff that you're going to learn from doing that, because of that pain you're producing, you're never going to want to replicate that pain. But don't let that pain stop you from doing. Just let it stop you from doing the same stupid shit over again.

BEN SETTLE: It's funny, you're like the vulgar Yoda. [laughing] It's all the same depth and stuff, but you just do it vulgar.

SHANE HUNTER: I spoke at that NES last year, and I was walking through the hotel to go speak, and saw on one of the little street kiosks – back to pattern interrupts here – that they had one of those girls, "Live, direct to your room, 1-800-XXX" shirts for sale in fluorescent orange. I was like, "Holy shit," so I grabbed that. It was like $20, so instead of wearing the typical stuff dress shirt and tie, I put this underneath the dress shirt. As soon as I got on stage, I think I dropped the F-bomb within the first three seconds, and then started stripping on stage to somewhat of a cheer. Then when I finally pulled that shirt, everyone was laughing, but now all the sudden everybody that was playing on their iPhones or doodling or falling asleep from the 87,000 hours of other presenters, all the sudden I had their attention.

That's the power of that pattern interrupt, but it's also the power of sometimes being vulgar. Frank Kern is one of the best with that. He'll drop the F-bomb in front of like 50,000 Christian doctors and they'll be like "What?!" but then the message that he follows with is so good that they forgive him for that. The fact is, he got their attention with that pattern interrupt. So that's why I cuss. It's not like I need to. I don't lack diction. It's just a thing. It's a pattern interrupt.

Chapter 12
How to Soak Your Business in New Leads, Prospects, and Sales Using Cheap, Simple-to-Write Pay-Per-View Ads

BEN SETTLE: I'm talking to Eric McMillan, someone I've been working closely with for the last year or two now. We've been playing with different niches and we finally narrowed it down to a couple. He's the traffic guy that I work with. I know nothing about traffic, but he knows traffic. I do conversion, he does the traffic. Specifically, he does this stuff called PPV – pay per view, is that what that stands for, Eric?

ERIC MCMILLAN: Yes, pay per view or it's sometimes called CPV, cost per view, same thing.

BEN SETTLE: I'm going to be learning along with everyone else reading this transcript because this is all new to me. I'm still trying to figure out AdWords, so that's where my mind is at. First of all, I want to talk a little about you and some of the things you've done, so when people are reading this transcript they know they're listening to someone who doesn't just talk the talk, but walks the walk. What got you started in all this internet stuff and traffic and all that sort of thing?

ERIC MCMILLAN: I have kind of an interesting story. It's a little parallel to yours, other than I picked the traffic path and you picked copywriting. Back in late 2008-2009 I had several successful construction companies and, to make a long story short, I ended up having to file personal bankruptcy. That got me looking for a way to make some money, so I joined a network marketing company, and then I got into this rabbit hole of internet marketing. All I heard was traffic, traffic, traffic, traffic, so I wanted to learn traffic.

More specifically, I like to think of myself as an expert in PPV. I'm sure there's a lot of people better than me at it, but I do okay. Most of what I do is lead gen stuff, but you can do straight-up conversions if you want to do that. It's just a little bit more tricky. You have to have a lot more pre-sell in place than if you just capture a lead and then sell them in the follow-up, which is probably what most of your guys will want to do.

BEN SETTLE: Yeah, these guys are mostly into conversion, and I'm in the same group. I want to build a list and use what I know to just sell the crap out of them.

ERIC MCMILLAN: This is definitely perfect. We can kind of move into exactly what PPV and CPV is, if you're good with that. Is that enough of a background for me?

BEN SETTLE: I want people to have some context, because they hear all these claims from people. Everybody pretends to be a traffic guy, but you really are out doing this. I don't know if you want to name people you've worked with or you've done client work or whatever, but what are some examples of some big traffic results you've had, just using this method?

ERIC MCMILLAN: Currently I'm the marketing manager for an information training company in the network marketing niche, and we do 350-400 leads a day, all pay per view. That's the in-house traffic that we run. We have affiliates, but I dwarf their traffic.

It's awesome to get leads, but the even better thing is we spend about $35 a customer and we make about $70 every customer that we get, so we're basically making 100% on our money. That's currently what I'm doing and the biggest niche I'm in. In the past I've done weight loss and have been about to get 15- to 20-cent leads, which is crazy in weight loss, and it's something you can be super-targeted with.

I think most people kind of avoid PPV a little bit because they don't understand it, or maybe they tried it or they hear horror stories about it, but if you really get in there it's just like any other traffic source. It's got its own unique parts about it, and once you understand that you can really crush it with this.

It's more geared towards mainstream stuff, like weight loss. It works with dating, as I'm finding out with a product you and I are working together on. You can't be demographically targeted with it, which makes it a little bit more difficult. You have

178

to be more selective with the sites you choose. Make money, obviously, insurance – any of that kind of stuff it definitely works with, and there's huge amounts of traffic.

BEN SETTLE: Mass market type stuff. I would love to get your opinion on something. When I think of mass market stuff for these types of things I think if there's a lot of TV advertising it would probably work for something like this, if it's being advertised on TV. Would that be accurate?

ERIC MCMILLAN: Yes and no. I think I say more mainstream stuff, meaning it's not going to work for a local business. It's not going to work for a brick and mortar that wants to get leads like in Gulf Shores, Alabama. It's not going to work for a business that's local here, but as long as it's a nationwide kind of thing and there's that demand where you can sell across the nation, then you can use PPV for it.

In weight loss, Weight Watchers is one that we crushed it with, popping up on Weight Watchers, because they do run ads. They have such huge reach, we basically just siphon traffic off of their huge ad budgets. The average cost per view – which is how you get billed with PPV – is going to be about 1.5 to 2 cents, so my ad gets shown to people for 1.5 to 2 cents. You think about that and you think about 12-cent leads, and that's pretty targeted. 20-cent leads are pretty targeted.

I think that's one of the common misconceptions. People think that it can only work for that big broad stuff. Sure, it can work for that but you've just got to realize there's a ton of competition for that kind of stuff too. The more niche you can be, as long as you can sell across the US – you can also sell in other countries with it, but I just haven't seen the huge volume like you get in the US with it.

BEN SETTLE: That's cool. So, let's go into what you wanted to go to earlier. Let's get real infantile here for people like me. Let's get down to the raw root of everything. What is PPV or CPV? Exactly what is it?

ERIC MCMILLAN: It's going to be user browser-based pop-ups, permission-based pop-ups. Here's the deal. These companies that have these PPV networks will go out and create a dating app or an app that goes in a web browser, not necessarily mobile. They don't have mobile traffic.

If you want to be able to have access to that game, that free PDF reader, whatever tool it is they develop, you have to agree to the terms of service. In the terms of service it says, "By checking this box that says I agree, you also agree to see occasional marketing messages daily," and that's what allows us to pop up on somebody's computer.

Now, if you and I were sitting next to each other and you had the pop-up toolbar installed and I didn't, and we went to the exact same website, you would see the ad and I wouldn't. It's not every single person that goes to a website that sees it. It's only those that are in the network's inventory that actually see the ad. Does that make sense?

BEN SETTLE: It does, yeah, definitely.

ERIC MCMILLAN: That's really how they go out and get the ad inventory. TrafficVance.com is one of the biggest players in that space, and they have a site called GameVance.com. You go there and if you want to play games – you just scroll through Facebook and you see all the damn games that people are playing all the time – if people want to download those games and be able to play them, they have to agree to download the game toolbar and that is how we're able to advertise to them.

There's TrafficVance and 50onRed.com. Those two are neck and neck, and they're relatively new, 50onRed, but their inventory is frickin' awesome and there's lots of buyers on it, which is a good thing. There's a couple others – LeadImpact, AdOnNetwork, and MediaTraffic. I kind of list those in order, I'd say. The best for me would be TrafficVance, 50onRed, LeadImpact being third, and then AdOnNetwork and MediaTraffic kind of tail out the end. If you've got a smaller budget you'll want to go to AdOn or MediaTraffic because they have a smaller buy-in.

LeadImpact, 50onRed, and Traffic Vance are all $1,000 to get started, then with TrafficVance you have to have a referral. You can't just go and sign up. You have to have a referral into the network.

BEN SETTLE: That would seem to be a good thing to keep the quality of advertisers in there. It's not like just anybody's going to be doing this, throwing crap out there and ruining it for everybody else's ads. Have you found that to be the case?

ERIC MCMILLAN: Yeah. LeadImpact used to be a $200 minimum buy-in. I've been doing PPV traffic for I'm going to say 4 years or maybe a little bit more than that. LeadImpact was pretty awesome because there were not very many people doing PPV at that time. It's been around for a long time, but people for whatever reason just stayed away from it. But they just recently went to $1,000 minimum buy-in and you can tell a huge difference, especially somebody like that that gets in there. If they're not a player that's going to constantly market, you can run them out of the bidding pretty quick.

Most of the bid systems, the average you'll pay, like I said, is 1.5 to 2 cents in the US to have one impression shown. You're charged on that stuff no matter whether they click on your ad or not. Every time the pop-up happens you're charged. That's why it's only a couple pennies to have that happen.

Pay per click, AdWords, that kind of stuff, every time somebody clicks on your ad is the only time you get charged, but you may be paying $1 to $2, depending what market you're in, to get one click.

BEN SETTLE: In your experience, how would you compare pay per click to pay per view to solo ads to email drops? Is this better than the other ones or is just dependent on what you're selling and how good you are at it? I guess here's my question – which gives you the best quality leads and which do you think is just overall better for someone who's technically challenged. Is this good for people who aren't real technical?

ERIC MCMILLAN: Oh yeah, traffic is traffic. You have to set up your capture pages and make sure all that stuff's working, no matter what traffic source you use. It's just a different modality that you have to learn. Really that just means the networks each have a little different back office.

But to answer your question, hands-down it's always been this way, it will always be this way – Google AdWords is the best traffic, no doubt. I would put PPV – and people would argue with me on this – in line with Facebook traffic as far as quality of leads you can get. I would put it above solo ads, and I've run a ton of solo traffic, and I know folks that really crush it with that. For me, you have to look at the kind of person that's going to be on those solo lists – mostly freebie seekers, and that's fine if you just want to build a list to build a list, but if you want to build a list to make money, you have to understand that going into it.

BEN SETTLE: This is kind of off-topic, but I recently ran a solo ad. The guy who's running the network is Igor, and he did his solo ad from his buyer's list, which I thought was a lot better than just going after a basic list of freebie people.

ERIC MCMILLAN: Yeah, they will do that, but you have to look at what did they buy in order to get on that buyer's list. The successful model in solo ads – and I know we're off-topic – but it's a super low-dollar front-end offer. Even $.99 would not be too low, because all you're trying to do is find out they have a credit card, and then you go and sell them something else. To move somebody up the ascension ladder there, the bottom rung of that ladder has to be super low.

BEN SETTLE: What about the copy for pay per view ads? Are there any tricks to that that you can share or is it just basic copywriting stuff? Anything interesting that you've found?

ERIC MCMILLAN: In the networking marketing/home business niche I'm in now – and this stayed true in weight loss a couple years ago when I was running a bunch of it; I was running green coffee CPA stuff – a big bold promise in the headline, call to action, and optin form is all I ran. It wasn't any fancy anything. It was all set up in Optimize Press and that was it.

I run a survey often right now also, and that thing does really well. You and I talked about this. I'm going through Ryan's course on Survey Funnels and I'll have to adapt what I do, because I don't give a crap about what they say in the survey right now, which I should. I just ask them questions to kind of pre-frame what they're about to see and get them to agree that that's what they want to see. That's the point of the survey, but you need to collect the data too and I've not been doing that because I'm lazy.

Those are the two kinds, just really simple. "Here's what I've got, here's how you get it, and put your name here," and that's it. That's all I really do.

BEN SETTLE: I'm intrigued by this survey thing. Do you remember basically what it says in the headline of your survey version? Does it just say, "Take this survey" or how would you word that, because I might actually try this. This is very interesting.

ERIC MCMILLAN: My headline is like, "Discover the simple way to recruit up to X number of reps per week into…." – actually, I changed that because we were getting slapped by a bunch of companies for using their names. It would be like, "Discover how to get to [whatever the top level is in that network marketing company] by recruiting up 240 reps per week, without harassing friends, family, or picking up the phone" – something along those lines, all three things that network marketers hate. Then the call to action is, "Take this simple survey to see if you have what it takes." That's the call to action, and then the questions start. I can send you an example of it.

The questions are like, "Do you fully believe in XYZ's products? Yes." They're all meant to be "yes" questions. "Do you believe there's a better way to become XYZ level in this company? Yes. Do you feel like your upline uses a different system and you'd like to learn that? Yes. Okay great, you're qualified. Opt in here to get this free report and I'll show you exactly how you can become XYZ in that company in the next 90 days."

BEN SETTLE: Let me ask you this question. I'm realizing that you're targeting network marketers, which is actually kind of specific. Let me ask this purely from a selfish point of view here. I sell email training. Would that work with pay per view? Would I be able to get traffic from established internet marketers who already know the basics of internet marketing, and they just want to get better at email? Is that something I should test, do you think?

ERIC MCMILLAN: Absolutely, you could do that. What comes to mind right off the bat – and you've have to obviously tailor it, and maybe even do some kind of pre-sell transition into what you do – but you could pop up on Aweber.com, GetResponse, Office Autopilot, Infusionsoft, and all these kinds of CRM autoresponders, and just make sure your message is specific to them. "Attention: Aweber Users. Discover the blah blah blah, how to 10X your money from email" or whatever.

BEN SETTLE: So in the back office you choose what sites it's going to be seen on?

ERIC MCMILLAN: Yeah. In order to set up a PPV campaign, you really just need the landing page that you're going to send traffic to, that's actually going to be whatever is going to pop up. You need a list of URLs or targets. You're bidding on URLs in this instance. For AdWords you'll bid on specific keywords. Say somebody searches *make money with email*, then your ad would show up.

In this instance, you would type *make money with email* into Google and you would see the first 10 sites that come up, and you would scrape those URLs. There's some tools that do it automated or you can do it manually, but you would use those URLs to kind of siphon the traffic off of Google. That's one method. Then obviously if you know competitors' URLs, you can pop up on them. If you know other tools specific to email marketing, you can pop up on those.

BEN SETTLE: This is so new to me. Even though you've been telling me about this for like the last two years, I haven't been paying attention. So, all these sites agree to be in these networks, is that how that works?

ERIC MCMILLAN: No, remember it's user browser based. It's the individual user's personal computer. They're the ones agreeing to see the marketing messages. Like if an Aweber user called them and said, "Hey, somebody's popping up on your site," they can contact me but I'll just be like, "I don't know what to tell you. It's the user agreeing to see it."

I've had that happen in the network marketing niche. They're like, "How do we stop these?" and I'm like, "You can't. It's user-based. The only way is to contact every single user that visits your site and tell them, 'Don't agree to download this toolbar,'" which is not going to happen.

BEN SETTLE: This is very interesting. I know these probably sound like very infantile questions, and they are, but I'm going to assume people reading this don't know anything about this either because we're all conversion people. We're not traffic people, so this is very interesting. I think this is going to help a lot of people. I can't wait to test this, man. You say there's a minimum buy-in, so you put in like say $1,000, and then that's what you have and they take money out as people see your ad? It's just deducted from that until you get down to 0?

ERIC MCMILLAN: Correct.

BEN SETTLE: Interesting.

ERIC MCMILLAN: There's some schools of thought on how you build out campaigns. I've always done it this way, and maybe it's wrong but it's worked for me. I always like to get a bunch of related URLs together. I'll scrape them from Google or YouTube, or you can scrape Amazon stuff if you want.

I like to use the analogy that it's like fishing. You don't know where you're going to get the bites because PPV is a little different, because not every single user has this toolbar installed. Let's say it's Aweber.com. Not every single visitor that goes to Aweber is going to have that toolbar, so is there enough traffic volume at Aweber to justify you building a separate campaign and a separate capture page that speaks exactly to those people? Those are the things I always like to find out initially.

It's like I'm throwing all these lines in the water, which means I'm putting pop-ups on all these URLs that I think might work, and then I'm just trying to find out where the bites are, which means where's the traffic volume at, especially if it's a brand new market.

BEN SETTLE: So in my case I would go to all these places where I know email marketers are. Some may bite and some may not, and the ones that don't, I just stop using those and just concentrate on the ones that do.

ERIC MCMILLAN: Yeah. Typically for me if I get to a site and if it's got X number of impressions, whatever that number is, in a short amount of time – if it's in 7 days and let's just say I get 1,000 impressions – maybe I didn't get any leads off it because my message is not tailored towards the specific people that are going to that site. I would take that URL and create a whole separate campaign and build a new lander using language specifically towards the people that are visiting that site. I would see if I could get it to convert into leads for me.

BEN SETTLE: And you can do as many as you want here. It's not like it costs you more. It's just that as see people see your ad, that's when they take money out of what you put in.

ERIC MCMILLAN: Right.

BEN SETTLE: Are you able to track these things to the sale by using tracking links, like 1ShoppingCart tracking links?

ERIC MCMILLAN: Yeah, you can actually track it. Like TrafficVance, for example, you can create a tracking pixel that you put on the thank you page or sales page, whichever page they go to right after they opt in. You can put a tracking pixel so it says, "Okay TrafficVance, this URL gave me a lead," so you know that XYZ URL gave you one lead at this cost.

Then you can take it one step further and say, "Hey, I want to create a purchase tracking pixel," and you put that on the thank you page after the purchase is confirmed, the credit card has gone through, and whatever page they're taken to. It's either the OTO or it's your thank-you page where you give them membership access, or whatever it is. You'll put that pixel there and it'll fire back and tell TrafficVance, "Okay, I just made a sale with this URL and this is the revenue that was generated from that sale," and it will assign it next to that. So you can actually track leads, cost per lead, and revenue and everything right there in TrafficVance. 50onRed does the same thing.

BEN SETTLE: How does that pixel work? Would you be putting like 12 pixels on that same page, or is it just one pixel that tracks everything in your account?

185

ERIC MCMILLAN: If you're using the same funnel, I would just obviously use one pixel. Let's say you run a bunch of traffic to 100 URLs and you find 2 or 3 that have a bunch of traffic and you want to break them out into their own campaigns, so you might craft a different headline on the sales page for each one of those different URLs.

I keep going back to Aweber and we'll keep using it. On the lander you might say, "Attention: Aweber users, blah blah blah I'm promising. To find out more [or whatever your call to action is going to be] enter your email here." Then they click through, opt in, and they see your thank-you page.

There you might have something that says, "If you're an Aweber user you don't want to miss this," and have an VSL or your sales letter or whatever you're going to have. You might custom tailor those things, but if you're just getting started I would just use the same thank you page and just have one pixel.

When you want to get really granular with it, yes, you definitely want to break it down and have separate pixels if you have a bunch of traffic. Like if you're spending $500 a day or $1,000 a day, you definitely want to have everything as granular as possible, because even a small incremental increase from one phrase on the thank you page makes a huge difference in revenue when you're running that kind of volume.

BEN SETTLE: That's very interesting. So, in my case, and anyone's case who's listening to this, they might be in something where they're not going to get that much traffic, especially starting right out, so we don't need to get too detailed like that. We can just put one pixel on it. By the way, what was that site where you have the pixel generated from again?

ERIC MCMILLAN: It's just the traffic network. It's TrafficVance.com.

BEN SETTLE: That's who you do your PPV through too? So they all have their own pixel? So it's not like a separate thing you've got to do. Okay. That's exciting, man.

ERIC MCMILLAN: Their tracking is pretty accurate. It's never going to be perfect. I use a 3rd party tracking software, CPV Lab, that I always track through. It's only because I'm anal and it's a failsafe for me. If their pixel doesn't fire, that pixel always fires for me, so I even know. If it doesn't catch the lead or the sale, I always have this failsafe that goes back and lets me know where it came from.

All we're doing is collecting data and making decisions based on the data we get. That's all we're doing. That's all traffic is.

BEN SETTLE: This is good, man, because I've been looking for a traffic source that fits for what I'm doing, and this would go for anyone who's reading this transcript, if they're in that intermediate stage where they're not going after someone who doesn't even know anything. They're going after someone who already has a certain set of knowledge and now they want to get better at what they already do, no matter what the niche is. It's hard to find that, at least I've been finding that to be the case.

In my case, I would have to start with people who've never even used email before. What's an autoresponder and blah blah blah. I don't want to go after those guys, even though that's probably a bigger market.

ERIC MCMILLAN: You can obviously test those things, and I have, like in weight loss especially. You might have a core group, because in weight loss – you've been in the market before – there's people that want to take a pill, don't want to do shit else, and they want to lose weight. There's people that have already done that and they feel like it's not going to work for them, so they want a meal plan. You can't talk to those people the same way if you're trying to sell them weight loss. You can't talk to them the same way. They're a different mentality.

It's like the get rich quick mentality in make money online stuff. You talk to those people differently than people that have already invested money in systems and courses and things like that, because they're just trying to figure out what the next piece is. It goes back to Marketing 101. You have to match up your message to your market. That's what it is.

BEN SETTLE: It always seems to go back to the fundamentals. I would like to kind of round this off with this one last question, a real recap. What order should we do things in? We go to XYZ site, we do XYZ thing first, and how do we get started on this, just as a recap?

ERIC MCMILLAN: If it were me just starting, I would go to www.50onRed.com and I'd get an account set up, because they don't require a referral. I would go through and scrape together – and scrape just means harvest or collect on a text or Notepad document – URLs that you're going to pop up on, because that's what the PPV network is going to read, the URL.

Again, you can bid on keywords, but in my experience the volume on the PPV side of things is not as big as it is just popping up on a specific URL, and it's also not as targeted. So get your list of URLs together.

Then you'll want to craft your capture page. Especially with the capture page, you've just got to understand that it's like any traffic. Getting started it's going to be the worst it's ever going to be. It can only get better from where you start, but you only do that by gathering that data and finding out specifically to PPV which URLs that you're bidding on actually have impressions.

It's even nicer if you get leads at that point, but you just have to understand, "Okay, I bid on a couple hundred URLs and I'm only having 4-5 that are giving me the bulk of impressions. The first thing is, is that URL who I'm looking to target?" If you get FoxNews.com and you're trying to sell email, yeah, they're going to have a ton of volume, but that's not who you're trying to target.

BEN SETTLE: I get it, okay.

ERIC MCMILLAN: If it's only 4 or 5, I would shut the rest of them off and I would focus in on those 4 or 5 that actually have traffic volume, and craft capture pages specifically to those, then let it run and see if you can get that traffic to convert for you.

Once you have it converting, then obviously the next step is you can go and optimize the thank you page to use language more specific for those specific URLs. It's the same thing – we're talking to conversion guys, but traffic is traffic is traffic.

BEN SETTLE: In other words, we don't want to get too bogged down with all this other. We just want to keep it simple to start out.

ERIC MCMILLAN: Exactly.

BEN SETTLE: That's like 3 steps. That's basically all we need to know to get started? That's excellent. Now, you mentioned that you could do a consult, like if people had questions about this they could pay you to consult with them on this. Are you doing that yet?

ERIC MCMILLAN: I do some monthly coaching that I have. I've got a couple guys I'm coaching right now, and it's good and it's bad. I like people that get results and that want results. I don't like people to pay me just to feel better about themselves. I want people that are actually action takers and do stuff.

BEN SETTLE: I call those guys investment-minded people versus opportunity-minded people. The people who are reading this should all be investment-minded people. I try very hard to not have the other type in there, so I think you're good to go.

ERIC MCMILLAN: That's the biggest thing. It's great to make some money, sure, it's great, but it's even better to get people in and actually have them get results. That's what I'm all about. I want people to get results. So yeah, I do coaching on a monthly basis. I only really have one level at this point. Like I said, it's not something that I actively go out and promote or anything like that.

BEN SETTLE: One last question and then I'm going to give your contact information. This kind of just popped in my head. How much time do you think it takes someone to just get something started, assuming they have their capture page and all that figured out, but just getting in there and learning everything, like the 50onRed one for example, getting that started? And what's the maintenance? Is it a lot of time that you put into it or is it just pretty quick?

ERIC MCMILLAN: That's going to depend, the amount of time. Optimizing stuff is going to depend on how many sites you're bidding on and what your budget is. Initially it's going to be a little more time. Let me just use this for an example. Right now, with 350 to 400 leads a day, at the point where I am with these, I have an outsourcer who does it but it takes them roughly 10-12 hours a week, but we're spending $7,000 to $8,000 a week in traffic.

If you're only running a couple campaigns, you're talking about an hour or two a week, and that's optimizing PPV but that's also looking at the landers. You're always split testing those, trying to make sure you can up conversions on them too, so a couple hours a week.

Getting set up, what I would do if you're going to go with 50onRed is I would create an account and get set up, and they will assign you an account manager. I would call them up or email and say, "Look man, I need you to help me set this up. I have no clue what I'm doing."

BEN SETTLE: I think that's a great idea. You just made it Ben-proof here. The last question is obviously if someone is interested in your coaching, what do they do next?

ERIC MCMILLAN: I would say use the email address info@eric-mcmillan.com. In the subject line put PPV coaching or something along those lines, just so I know that it's something I need to look at.

BEN SETTLE: I really appreciate you doing this. In Email Players we're all about conversion, but very few of us are good at the traffic part. Those who are good at the traffic part are just killing it, of course, and the rest of us would like to get up to their speed as far as driving traffic. So, thanks, man, I appreciate it.

ERIC MCMILLAN: Not a problem. I hope it was helpful and I didn't get too many people's eyes crossed.

BEN SETTLE: Not at all, man. You kept this Ben-proof. I guarantee you, if I can figure it out, they can, so it's all good. We'll talk to you soon. Bye.

Disclosures and Disclaimers

All trademarks and service marks are the properties of their respective owners. All references to these properties are made solely for editorial purposes. Except for marks actually owned by the Author or the Publisher, no commercial claims are made to their use, and neither the Author nor the Publisher is affiliated with such marks in any way.

Unless otherwise expressly noted, none of the individuals or business entities mentioned herein has endorsed the contents of this book.

Limits of Liability & Disclaimers of Warranties

Because this book is a general educational information product, it is not a substitute for professional advice on the topics discussed in it.

The materials in this book are provided "as is" and without warranties of any kind either express or implied. The Author and the Publisher disclaim all warranties, express or implied, including, but not limited to, implied warranties of merchantability and fitness for a particular purpose. The Author and the Publisher do not warrant that defects will be corrected, or that any website or any server that makes this book available is free of viruses or other harmful components. The Author does not warrant or make any representations regarding the use or the results of the use of the materials in this book in terms of their correctness, accuracy, reliability, or otherwise. Applicable law may not allow the exclusion of implied warranties, so the above exclusion may not apply to you.

Under no circumstances, including, but not limited to, negligence, shall the Author or the Publisher be liable for any special or consequential damages that result from the use of, or the inability to use this book, even if the Author, the Publisher, or an authorized representative has been advised of the possibility of such damages. Applicable law may not allow the limitation or exclusion of liability or incidental or consequential damages, so the above limitation or exclusion may not apply to you. In no event shall the Author or Publisher total liability to you for all damages, losses, and causes of action (whether in contract, tort, including but not limited to, negligence or otherwise) exceed the amount paid by you, if any, for this book.

You agree to hold the Author and the Publisher of this book, principals, agents, affiliates, and employees harmless from any and all liability for all claims for damages due to injuries, including attorney fees and costs, incurred by you or caused to third parties by you, arising out of the products, services, and activities discussed in this book, excepting only claims for gross negligence or intentional tort.

You agree that any and all claims for gross negligence or intentional tort shall be settled solely by confidential binding arbitration per the American Arbitration Association's commercial arbitration rules. All arbitration must occur in the municipality where the Author's principal place of business is located. Arbitration fees and costs shall be split equally, and you are solely responsible for your own lawyer fees.

Facts and information are believed to be accurate at the time they were placed in this book. All data provided in this book is to be used for information purposes only. The information contained within is not intended to provide specific legal, financial, tax, physical or mental health advice, or any other advice whatsoever, for any individual or company and should not be relied upon in that regard. The services described are only offered in jurisdictions where they may be legally offered. Information provided is not all-inclusive, and is limited to information that is made available and such information should not be relied upon as all-inclusive or accurate.

For more information about this policy, please contact the Author at the e-mail address listed in the Copyright Notice at the front of this book.

IF YOU DO NOT AGREE WITH THESE TERMS AND EXPRESS CONDITIONS, DO NOT READ THIS BOOK. YOUR USE OF THIS book, PRODUCTS, SERVICES, AND ANY PARTICIPATION IN ACTIVITIES MENTIONED IN THIS book, MEAN THAT YOU ARE AGREEING TO BE LEGALLY BOUND BY THESE TERMS.

Affiliate Compensation & Material Connections Disclosure

This book may contain hyperlinks to websites and information created and maintained by other individuals and organizations. The Author and the Publisher do not control or guarantee the accuracy, completeness, relevance, or timeliness of any information or privacy policies posted on these linked websites.

You should assume that all references to products and services in this book are made because material connections exist between the Author or Publisher and the providers of the mentioned products and services ("Provider"). You should also assume that all hyperlinks within this book are affiliate links for (a) the Author, (b) the Publisher, or (c) someone else who is an affiliate for the mentioned products and services (individually and collectively, the "Affiliate").

The Affiliate recommends products and services in this book based in part on a good faith belief that the purchase of such products or services will help readers in general.

The Affiliate has this good faith belief because (a) the Affiliate has tried the product or service mentioned prior to recommending it or (b) the Affiliate has researched the reputation of the Provider and has made the decision to recommend the Provider's products or services based on the Provider's history of providing these or other products or services.

The representations made by the Affiliate about products and services reflect the Affiliate's honest opinion based upon the facts known to the Affiliate at the time this book was published.

Because there is a material connection between the Affiliate and Providers of products or services mentioned in this book, you should always assume that the Affiliate may be biased because of the Affiliate's relationship with a Provider and/or because the Affiliate has received or will receive something of value from a Provider.

Perform your own due diligence before purchasing a product or service mentioned in this book.

The type of compensation received by the Affiliate may vary. In some instances, the Affiliate may receive complimentary products (such as a review copy), services, or money from a Provider prior to mentioning the Provider's products or services in this book.

In addition, the Affiliate may receive a monetary commission or non-monetary compensation when you take action by clicking on a hyperlink in this book. This includes, but is not limited to, when you purchase a product or service from a Provider after clicking on an affiliate link in this book.

Earnings & Income Disclaimers

No Earnings Projections, Promises or Representations

For purposes of these disclaimers, the term "Author" refers individually and collectively to the author of this book and to the affiliate (if any) whose affiliate links are embedded in this book.

You recognize and agree that the Author and the Publisher have made no implications, warranties, promises, suggestions, projections, representations or guarantees whatsoever to you about future prospects or earnings, or that you will earn any money, with respect to your purchase of this book, and that the Author and the Publisher have not authorized any such projection, promise, or representation by others.

Any earnings or income statements, or any earnings or income examples, are only estimates of what you *might* earn. There is no assurance you will do as well as stated in any examples. If you rely upon any figures provided, you must accept the entire risk of not doing as well as the information provided. This applies whether the earnings or income examples are monetary in nature or pertain to advertising credits which may be earned (whether such credits are convertible to cash or not).

There is no assurance that any prior successes or past results as to earnings or income (whether monetary or advertising credits, whether convertible to cash or not) will apply, nor can any prior successes be used, as an indication of your future success or results from any of the information, content, or strategies. Any and all claims or representations as to income or earnings (whether monetary or advertising credits, whether convertible to cash or not) are not to be considered as "average earnings".

Testimonials & Examples

Testimonials and examples in this book are exceptional results, do not reflect the typical purchaser's experience, do not apply to the average person and are not intended to represent or guarantee that anyone will achieve the same or similar results. Where specific income or earnings (whether monetary or advertising credits, whether convertible to cash or not), figures are used and attributed to a specific individual or business, that individual or business has earned that amount. There is no assurance that you will do as well using the same information or strategies. If you rely on the specific income or earnings figures used, you must accept all the risk of not doing as well. The described experiences are atypical. Your financial results are likely to differ from those described in the testimonials.

The Economy

The economy, where you do business, on a national and even worldwide scale, creates additional uncertainty and economic risk. An economic recession or depression might negatively affect your results.

Your Success or Lack of It

Your success in using the information or strategies provided in this book depends on a variety of factors. The Author and the Publisher have no way of knowing how well you will do because they do not know you, your background, your work ethic, your dedication, your motivation, your desire, or your business skills or practices. Therefore, neither the Author nor the Publisher guarantees or implies that you will get rich, that you will do as well, or that you will have any earnings (whether monetary or advertising credits, whether convertible to cash or not), at all.

Businesses and earnings derived therefrom involve unknown risks and are not suitable for everyone. You may not rely on any information presented in this book or otherwise provided by the Author or the Publisher, unless you do so with the knowledge and understanding that you can experience significant losses (including, but not limited to, the loss of any monies paid to purchase this book and/or any monies spent setting up, operating, and/or marketing your business activities, and further, that you may have no earnings at all (whether monetary or advertising credits, whether convertible to cash or not).

Forward-Looking Statements

Materials in this book may contain information that includes or is based upon forward-looking statements within the meaning of the securities litigation reform act of 1995. Forward-looking statements give the Author's expectations or forecasts of future events. You can identify these statements by the fact that they do not relate strictly to historical or current facts. They use words such as "anticipate," "estimate," "expect," "project," "intend," "plan," "believe," and other words and terms of similar meaning in connection with a description of potential earnings or financial performance.

Any and all forward-looking statements here or on any materials in this book are intended to express an opinion of earnings potential. Many factors will be important in determining your actual results and no guarantees are made that you will achieve results similar to the Author or anybody else. In fact, no guarantees are made that you will achieve any results from applying the Author's ideas, strategies, and tactics found in this book.

Purchase Price

Although the Publisher believes the price is fair for the value that you receive, you understand and agree that the purchase price for this book has been arbitrarily set by the Publisher. This price bears no relationship to objective standards.

Due Diligence

You are advised to do your own due diligence when it comes to making any decisions. Use caution and seek the advice of qualified professionals before acting upon the contents of this book or any other information. You shall not consider any examples, documents, or other content in this book or otherwise provided by the Author or Publisher to be the equivalent of professional advice.

The Author and the Publisher assume no responsibility for any losses or damages resulting from your use of any link, information, or opportunity contained in this book or within any other information disclosed by the Author or the Publisher in any form whatsoever.

YOU SHOULD ALWAYS CONDUCT YOUR OWN INVESTIGATION (PERFORM DUE DILIGENCE) BEFORE BUYING PRODUCTS OR SERVICES FROM ANYONE OFFLINE OR VIA THE INTERNET. THIS INCLUDES PRODUCTS AND SERVICES SOLD VIA HYPERLINKS EMBEDDED IN THIS BOOK.

50937972R00116